Discovering the Faith

John Pritchard

Wyche Publications
Woodlands
Eaton Road
Malvern Wells
Worcs WR14 4PE

Printed and bound in Great Britain by:
Page Bros
Mile Cross Lane
Norwich
Norfolk NR6 6SA

ISBN   0-9506462-1-0

DISTRIBUTED BY:
Additional Curates Society
Gordon Browning House
8 Spitfire Road
Birmingham
B24 9PB

Tel: 0121 382 5533
Fax: 0121 382 6999

FRONT COVER
The Church has been called "the Ship of Salvation". We come on board
through the waters of Baptism. Hopefully, we change from being
passengers to crew members on the exciting journey of "Discovering the
Faith". Our destination is the Heavenly City.

*This book is dedicated to
the faithful congregation
of
Emmanuel Church, Sutton Coldfield
with whom the author was privileged
to spend the last ten years of his ministry.*

INTRODUCTION AND THANKS

The Aim of the Book. The Christian Faith has been altered, watered down and re-introduced by modern liberals. The aim of this book is to re-state the traditional faith as it has been accepted through the centuries. It is written in a form which is easy to read and understand.

Christianity is a large and complicated subject. Much more could have been written about each section. Perhaps the book will inspire the reader to further study – and a leap in faith?

About the book. A vast number of books have been written about the Christian Faith. The basic thoughts in this book are not new. They rely largely on what others have discovered and written. It is a re-statement of the traditional teaching of the Church through the ages.

The Ordination of Women. The Church of England decided to ordain women to the Priesthood. This is still a controversial issue. Some accept this new ministry, and others reject it. The Church has made mistakes in the past. If the ordination of women is from God, it will succeed. If it is of human origin, it will fail. We must not forget that we are in "a period of discernment". Four pages are included on this important subject to help each reader to make up his or her mind.

How to use the book: "Discovering the Faith" is a short account of a very large subject. Hopefully this simple introduction will encourage you to find the love of God in Jesus Christ in regular worship. Some may find it a good exercise to read only one chapter per day.

We are all searching. You cannot learn to swim without getting into the water. So with the faith. We are all making a spiritual journey or pilgrimage throughout life. The early Christians were called followers of 'The Way'. Jeremiah wrote: "Thus says the Lord: 'Stand by the (cross) roads, and ask for the ancient paths, where the good way is; and walk in it, and find rest for your souls'." (Jeremiah 6.16). Six hundred years later, Jesus said "I am the Way, the Truth and the Life". (St John 14.6). Sadly, many have left these "ancient paths" today.

Thank you. I am grateful for help received from many, including – The Venerable George Austin, well known writer and broadcaster, and the former Archdeacon of York – for the Foreword. The Right Revd John Broadhurst, Bishop of Fulham – for the Commendation. The Revd Dr Geoffrey Kirk. The Additional Curates Society and the Revd Stephen Leach, Mr Robert Jordan and Mr John Kearney. Also all who have helped me to grow in the faith over the years.

Scripture quotations are from Revised Standard Version of the Bible.

I hope you find the book is helpful.

John Pitchford

CONTENTS

CONTENTS

DISCOVERING THE FAITH

WHY BELIEVE IN GOD?

God is Spirit. He does not exist in time or space. Thus you cannot touch, measure or weigh God, nor carry out any scientific tests. Many scientists do believe in God and are practising Christians. But no one can "prove" or "disprove" that God exists. We can only say "It is probable that God exists". This does make sense of all the facts.

Cause and effect. The universe does exist! Where did it come from? Was it an accident, or chance happening? Or did "Someone" cause it to come into existence? There is no effect without a cause. God is the "first cause" of all that exists.

The Mind or Designer who planned the universe. The universe is a unity which fits together in one complete whole. There are signs of design and order in the universe. The tide ebbs and flows in a regular pattern. The four seasons come year after year. Consider the fine details of the human mind. It is unlikely that the brain developed just by chance through evolution. It is more probable there is a "Mind" or "Designer" who planned and created the universe, and who keeps it all in existence. This Creative Mind, or Creator, is a Person called God.

Goodness, beauty, truth and love. From where do these qualities come? People see God in what is good, and beautiful and true. These precious qualities did not just develop out of thin air over the centuries. They exist because God Himself is the source of all these gifts. They are reflections of His unimaginable glory.

Persecution and the martyrs. Many followers of Jesus died as martyrs during the Roman Empire and in the centuries since then. There have been many martyrs of other world religions. All these died because of their belief in the existence of God.

God has "revealed" Himself to us. There is a remarkable collection of documents ("books") in the Bible. They were all written by people who had been deeply affected by their experiences of God. This includes the Patriarchs (Abraham, Isaac and Jacob) and the Prophets. The Divine Revelation includes the coming of God's only Son, Jesus Christ, and the Gospels and Letters written about Him. Some books are difficult to understand; some are about "blood and thunder". However, all the books do point towards the existence of God. The Bible does not try to prove the existence of God: it accepts Him as a fact of life. The wisdom and the experience of past ages should not be dismissed too easily.

Belief through the ages. All through recorded history, a very large majority of people have believed in God. Sadly, many people today do not make time even to think about God, except perhaps in times of crisis.

Spiritual experiences. God has been experienced in the Christian Church through the centuries. The NT gives an account of those who put their trust in God through Jesus Christ. Their experience of God is part of the continuing life of the Church.

Countless Christians still do worship and pray to God Sunday by Sunday. Are all these people mistaken? Add to this all the Hindus, Muslims, Sikhs, Buddhists, Jews and others. All of them believe that God does exist – even if there are differences of opinion about the nature of God.

The problem of evil and suffering. Those who do not believe in God may argue like this: If God is good and loving and all-powerful, why does He allow evil and suffering in the world? Evil is in our hearts. We often chose evil instead of good. To remove free will would make us robots. Jesus died on the Cross to free us from the power of sin and evil. His death and resurrection give us a powerful answer to this problem.

Supernatural experiences. Believers and non-believers have supernatural experiences. Some of them may be caused by illness, drugs or hallucinations. Others may be genuine experiences of God.

The "Moral Argument" for the existence of God. Where do human beings get a sense of right and wrong? Christians believe that this does not come from evolution but from God.

In all these thoughts, we stand at the edge of a mystery. God may be "hidden" – but He has left many clues or footsteps to help us to find Him. There are good reasons why we can believe in God. Taken together, they present a good case.

WHAT IS GOD LIKE?

Our image of God is vital. What sort of God do you pray to and worship? A God who forces and compels or who attracts you? Some people have a harmful image of God. An important part of the spiritual journey is to correct false ideas. He can never be adequately expressed in words or definitions. There is no clear and simple description of Him in the Bible. What we know of Him is what He has communicated or "revealed" to us through the Bible and the Church. At the fullness of time, God revealed Himself to us more fully in Jesus. These revelations only point us to the truth. "Now we see in a mirror dimly, but then (after death) face to face." (1 Corinthians 13.12)

"He who has seen me has seen the Father." (St John 14.9). Jesus shows us what God is like. He points us to God the Father.

God is a Person. (See "The Holy Trinity" pages 8-9). We can know God in an intimate and personal way through prayer and worship But God can also seem to be hidden, invisible and mysterious.

God is a Spirit. We should say, the Supreme Spirit. God alone is perfect. He is holy and good, and just and merciful.

God alone is self-existent. He was not created by anyone. Material things all come to an end, but God will have no end, just as He had no beginning. God is eternal. God is all-sufficient in Himself. He is independent. All created things and beings depend on God for their existence. God depends on no one.

God is greater than all these descriptions. Yet He is very real. We can pray to God, and have a close and personal relationship with Him through our prayers, the Eucharist and the Bible.

There is only one God. The Jews came to realise that their God was the only God. All other "gods" were false, and man-made idols. The one true God is unique. There can only be one God. When the Jews understood there was only one God, then God revealed to them more about His nature as the Holy Trinity.

God is our Father. Jesus taught us to call God "our Father". We are His sons and daughters. We enter this relationship through Baptism. He is not a remote, uncaring or harsh Father (like some human fathers). God cares for us and loves us, whatever we do. He is a God who forgives all our sins, when we are sorry and ask for forgiveness.

God is a Suffering God. He allowed His Son to suffer and die for us. He allows Himself to suffer with us and for us today when we sin.

God is Almighty. All energy and power in the universe ultimately come from God. God "emptied" Himself of His power when He "took flesh" in Jesus. He showed His power in raising Jesus from the dead. God has unlimited power, but He does not force His will on us. In the mystery of His love, He exercises His power through weakness.

God is our Judge. Christ "will come again to judge the living and the dead." (Creed). This side of God's character is often forgotten. But God is merciful, and He forgives us if we turn to Him in penitence and faith.

God is Light. 1 John 1.5: "God is light. In Him is no darkness at all." God "lives in unapproachable light". (1 Timothy 6.16).

God is Creator of the universe. God alone is not created by anyone. He has existed from all eternity. God did not need to create the universe. He is self-sufficient. He created the universe to share His goodness with other people. God is present in His creation. He is all around us. Nothing existed, and then at the beginning of time, God created the universe out of nothing. God is creator of all that we can see, and also of the unseen spiritual world.

The anger and love of God. There are some barbaric passages in the OT. God is angry when the Israelites betray Him, act unjustly, or are unfaithful and "go after other gods". The writers saw God's reaction in disaster. God is our Judge, but also a God of love and forgiveness. This is seen in parables such as the Lost Sheep or the Prodigal Son.

God is a seeking God. He does not force Himself on us. But He is ever seeking us, and our response to His love in Jesus.

God is a giving God. He loved the world so much that He gave His only Son. He gives us all that we have. In return, He wants our love.

FAITH

What is Faith? The word "Faith" is not easy to define. It has two different meanings – "belief" and "trust".

(1) Faith means the beliefs and teachings of the Church, found in the Bible, the three Creeds (See pages 90-91) and the Seven Councils of the Church (See page 35).

(2) God has taken the initiative and reached out to us in Jesus Christ. He invites us to respond to His love. He invites us to put our trust in His mercy and forgiveness. "Faith" is God's free gift to all who actively accept and put their trust in Him. Together with "hope" and "love", faith is one of the three "Theological Virtues".

How do we find a personal Faith? We cannot come to faith in God by our own efforts. God seeks us. He wants us to turn to Him. People become aware of their need for God for different reasons.

Faith is not about proof. It is not a leap in the dark. It is more a coming into the light of God's truth. Faith comes as a result of hearing the Word of God.

We come to faith through the work and action of the Holy Spirit on our minds and souls. Even so, putting our trust in God in this way involves a genuine human response. Our minds and wills freely co-operate with God's plan. God gives us faith. He "infuses" faith into our souls. It is His free gift to all who put their trust in Him.

Faith is given to us before we understand it fully. It does involve knowing with our mind, and accepting the truth of the Gospel. Our minds and wills respond and co-operate with the Holy Spirit. We become aware of our sins and repent. We seek God's will in our lives. We are invited to love God, and to love our neighbour. You cannot separate faith from love. Faith without "good works" is dead.

Coming to faith in God is like sowing a seed. The time scale differs from person to person. Some seeds need a long time to germinate and grow in the dark before coming to the surface. For others, the "conversion" process does not take so long (like Saul [St Paul] on the Road to Damascus?). We can pray for faith, even if we have doubts. The Holy Spirit helps us to accept the truths about God.

Problems with Faith. Some people are brought up in a Christian family, and this can give security and strength for their faith. For others, faith does not come easily or naturally. It can be a struggle and a testing time, with questioning and doubt. Two examples of these questions: If God is a God of love, why does He allow so much evil and suffering in the world? (See pages 116-117). How far can we trust the Bible? (See pages 22-23). It is wise to face doubts and questions, and to make sure that our faith is honest, and not based on a pretence. As St Paul said: "know the reason for the hope that is in you." Our understanding of Jesus can be deepened through dealing with such problems.

Some have doubts about God because He does not immediately answer their prayers. God might answer your prayer with a simple – No. Or not yet. Prayer has to be made in accordance with God's will, not ours. "Thy will be done, on earth as it is in Heaven."

Many have found encouragement in the words of St Mark 9.24: "Lord, I believe. Help thou mine unbelief."

How do we grow in Faith? Putting our trust in God is only the first step. There is a long journey of discovery ahead in terms of spiritual growth and learning the faith. This is sometimes called "Christian formation".

Before we come to faith, the faith of the Church is already there to help us on our pilgrimage. We are united with Christ through Baptism. We learn about the ways of God and the unseen spiritual world through prayer, reading the Bible and the Eucharist. Thus our faith is increased, and we become less self-centred and more God-centred in our lives.

Faith is a gift from God. We believe that all people are made in the image of God, and that God loves all people equally. Some accept God's free gift of faith, while others reject it, or are completely indifferent. For those who accept it, it is good to give thanks to God regularly for His gift to us (and for our Baptism). It is also good to reflect on the story of our own faith development – and to consider how much doubt has been a part of our spiritual journey. Hebrews 11.1: "Faith is the assurance of things hoped for, the conviction of things not seen."

THE HOLY TRINITY

The Holy Trinity. Cardinal John Henry Newman clearly states the Christian view of God in his lovely hymn – "Firmly I believe and truly, God is three and God is one".

The Trinity is very difficult to understand. Why do we need to believe that "God is three and God is one"? Belief in the Trinity came from the experience of Christians, and the writings of the New Testament.

God is One. Most religions at the time of Jesus believed there were many "gods". (Polytheism). The Jews passionately believed in only one God. Deuteronomy 6.4: "Hear, O Israel: The Lord our God is one Lord." Christians (and Muslims) share this belief with the Jews that there is only one God. Belief in only one God (called Monotheism) is an essential part of the Christian religion.

The Christian view of God is different from the views of all the other world religions.

Development of the Trinity. The early Church came to believe that there are three "Persons" in one God. This doctrine was slowly worked out at the great Ecumenical Councils of the Church, at Nicaea in 325AD, Constantinople in 381AD, and Chalcedon in 451AD. The Trinity was included in the Creeds, and it is a basic part of the faith.

Belief that the Father is God. There is no doubt that God the Father is truly God. St John 8.41: "We have one Father, even God."
The Lord's Prayer – "Our Father, who art in Heaven ..."

Belief that Jesus Christ is God. The Nicene Creed (used in the Eucharist) – makes a tremendous claim about Jesus Christ. He is "the only begotten Son of God, begotten of His Father before all worlds, God of God, Light of Light, very God of very God, begotten not made, being of one substance with the Father". This belief came only after a long period of conflict and debate. Behind those words there is the story of how the Holy Spirit guided the Church into the way of truth.

The first disciples realised that Jesus Christ was more than just a man. The Scriptures clearly state that He is also divine (ie He is God). The "Word" and "Christ" are different ways of understanding Jesus:

8

St John 1.1: "In the beginning was the Word, and the Word was with God, and the Word was God."
St John 20.28: Thomas said to Jesus, "My Lord and my God."

The miracles supported the early Christian view that Jesus was more than just a man. His Resurrection from the dead confirmed their belief that He was God.

The Holy Spirit is God. After Christ returned to Heaven, His presence was still experienced by the disciples. The Holy Spirit changed the lives of the disciples. Because of this experience, they came to realise that the Holy Spirit is also God.

The Trinity in Baptism. From earliest times, the Trinity has been used in Baptism. St Matthew 28.19: Jesus said … "Baptising them in the name of the Father and of the Son and of the Holy Spirit."

The three "Persons". God is in some ways a mystery, but He is not an impersonal force. We can get to know God as a person or three Persons. But there are not three different Gods, but three Persons in one God. "Person" is the most suitable word which could be found to describe such a mystery, which will always be beyond human thought. The three Persons are one in action, power and glory.

The Trinity is a community of love. There is a perfect relationship and common fellowship between Father, Son and Holy Spirit. It is a sharing of a life of love. Every Christian who is in a right relationship with God can share in the community of love of the Blessed Trinity.

The three Persons are distinct from each other, but equal. Each has certain qualities which are different from the qualities of the other two Persons. They share a common "substance." Again, no better word has been found than substance.

The mystery of God's nature. God revealed Himself as Father, Son and Holy Spirit. The Trinity is the best way we can find to describe the mystery of God. It is a vital part of our prayer and worship. We pray to the Father, through the Son, and in the Spirit. Belief in the Holy Trinity is the basic foundation of Christianity.

CREATION

Some people believe that Science has disproved religion. For some, the subject of creation is an on-going battleground between religion and science. For others, the wonders of creation and science go hand in hand, each enhancing the other.

Creation in the Old Testament. In the early chapters of Genesis, there are two different accounts. The details do not always agree. In the first (Genesis 1.1-2.4) – man and woman were created together. Genesis 1.27: "God created man in His own image, in the image of God He created him; male and female He created them."

In the second account, God makes man from the dust and breathes life into his nostrils. Then the woman is made out of a rib taken from the man. Genesis 2.18: "It is not good that the man should be alone; I will make a helper fit for him."

Nobody was present when God created the universe. The people who wrote about creation in Genesis looked at the world, and some deep questions came into their minds. "Where did it all come from?" "Who was the Creator?" They tried to make sense of it by writing two beautiful stories. Genesis 1 and 2 are sometimes called parables or myths. Genesis 1 was written during or after the Exile (586-539BC) and Genesis 2 was written four centuries earlier. They are the best explanation that the writers could produce at the time. They are important because they tell us that God alone created the universe.

Adam and Eve. "Fundamentalists" are Christians who believe that the whole of the Bible is literally true. They believe that God made two people called Adam and Eve, and that He created the world in six days, as recorded in Genesis. Most Christians, however, do not accept the details of Genesis as an a accurate description of what happened. The stories in Genesis tell us *who* created the universe – namely God. Genesis does not tell us *how* the world was created. That is the job of the scientists. The discoveries of science only enhance the marvel of God's creation.

Charles Darwin. In 1859, Darwin published a book on his research into fossils. It was called "The Origin of Species by Means of Natural Selection". His theory of evolution gave a very different version from the Book of Genesis. As a result, many people now believe that science has disproved religion.

Scientific View of Creation and Evolution. A simple summary goes something like this – The universe came into existence thousands of millions of years ago with a Big Bang. No one understands how it came to happen. Evolution was a very long process over millions of years. Natural selection leads to the survival of the fittest. Tiny micro-organisms changed and evolved into plants and animals. Human beings developed from bacteria. The whole universe is continually expanding into infinite space.

Science is not interested in questions such as "who" made the universe, and "why?" Science likes to examine facts – and then put forward a theory which can be tested by experiments. The whole idea of "purpose" is outside the work of science.

A Christian view of Creation. The universe did not always exist. It was created by God, out of nothing, at the beginning of time. God is the Supreme Spirit, and God alone exists in Himself. God alone can create. God did not need to create the universe. He made it so that He could share His love and goodness with us. He created the visible and the invisible world, including the angels and spiritual beings.

Many scientists today do actually believe in God. Many are practising Christians. (There is, in fact, a Society of Ordained Scientists).

As a result of scientific research, we now have a much clearer understanding of how the world was made and evolved. But this does not dispense with the "Person" who created it. Science is not the only way to discover what is true.

In the light of Darwin's discoveries, it is perfectly reasonable to believe in God as the Creator. He has a purpose for His creation. This purpose is shown to us – not through science – but through history, and in the person of Jesus Christ.

The scientific and Christian view of creation can surely exist advantageously side by side.

MAIN EVENTS IN THE OLD TESTAMENT

Scholars may disagree about the dates of some of the events in the OT.

1800BC Abraham. Jews, Christians and Muslims all look back to Abraham for the beginning of their religion. God made himself known to Abraham, and "called" him to leave the Fertile Crescent (Persia now called Iraq) God promised to make Abraham's descendants a great nation, and give them their own country (The Promised Land). Abraham's son was Isaac. His son was Jacob (also called Israel). Jacob had twelve sons – the ancestors of the Twelve Tribes of Israel.

1700BC Slavery in Egypt. During a time of famine, the Twelve Tribes went to Egypt for food. In the course of time, they became slaves for the Egyptians.

1250BC The Exodus. Moses led the Israelites out of slavery in Egypt to freedom through the Dead Sea. A Covenant was made between God and the Israelites at Mount Sinai. The Ten Commandments were the result of this Covenant.

Entering the Promised Land. After forty years wandering in the desert, the Israelites began to fight their way into Canaan. It was a series of small invasions, and Joshua was one of the main leaders.

1220 – 1030BC The Judges. "The Judges" were military leaders who organised informal groupings of the tribes to fight the Philistines and the Canaanites, and other people living there.

1030 – 1010BC King Saul. He was anointed by the Prophet Samuel as the first king. The 12 tribes had a loose kind of unity under Saul.

1010 – 970BC King David. A brilliant ruler and soldier, he completed the conquest of the country, and Jerusalem became his capital. The Ark of the Covenant (containing the Ten Commandments) was brought to Jerusalem. Israel's hope of a Saviour (Messiah) was to come from the "House and lineage of David".

970 – 930BC King Solomon. He was David's son and built the First Temple at Jerusalem. His reign was called "the Golden Age" (perhaps connected with the achievements of his father, David?).

930 – 722BC The Divided Kingdom. After Solomon's death, the country was divided into Israel (the ten Tribes) in the North, and Judah and Benjamin in the South.

740 – 700BC The Prophet Isaiah in Judah.

721BC The Assyrians destroyed the Northern Kingdom – Israel.
All traces of the ten northern Tribes completely disappear from history.

626 – 585BC The Prophet Jeremiah in Judah.

586BC Jerusalem captured by the Babylonians. The Temple was destroyed and the Jews were taken into captivity. This "Exile" in Babylon lasted 70 years. "A Faithful Remnant" stayed loyal to God during the Exile. They began to think in terms of a Messiah who would restore the former glory of King David's reign. The Suffering Servant Songs come from this period. (Isaiah 42.1-9; 49.1-9; 50.4-9; 52.13-53.12).

539BC "The Return". The Persians were now the world power, and King Cyrus allowed the Jews to return to their own country. In due course, they re-built the Temple at Jerusalem (Second Temple). The leaders at this time were Ezra and Nehemiah.

331 – 323BC Palestine controlled by the Greeks. Alexander the Great had defeated the Persians. He died suddenly at an early age. The Greeks ruled the country.

323 – 198BC Palestine ruled by the Ptolemies of Egypt.

198 – 166BC The country was ruled by Syria. (Greek Kings called the Seleucids). They tried to impose Greek customs and to destroy the Jewish religion. Judas Maccabaeus led a rebellion against this. After twenty years of guerrilla warfare, the Syrians gave them independence

166 – 63BC The Israelites became independent again. They were allowed to rule themselves under their own High Priest.

63BC Jerusalem captured by the Romans. The country became part of the Roman Empire. Puppet Kings were set up eg. King Herod.

THE CONTENTS OF THE OLD TESTAMENT

The OT is regularly used in public worship and private devotion. Thus it is helpful to have a good understanding of this magnificent inheritance. The OT is a library of 39 books. It is mainly about God's relationship with the Jews over a period of 1,000 years, dating from about 1,100BC to 150BC. No other nation has such a unique collection of sacred writings.

The Old Testament is the Jewish Bible, and was written in Hebrew (the language of the Israelites). It was the Bible used and loved by Jesus. There are three main divisions in the Old Testament – (1) The Law (Torah), (2) The Prophets and (3) The Writings.

Pre-History Folk Tales and Legends. Primitive people did not understand certain matters, so they invented folk tales to explain them. These include such stories as Adam and Eve, The Great Flood and the Tower of Babel, which are recorded mainly in Genesis.

Jewish History begins with Abraham. God called Abraham to leave his native country and go to a foreign land. He was to set himself apart from other nations. The reason for this is simple – God promised that all nations would be blessed through Abraham and his descendants. The Jews were God's "Chosen People" called to prepare for the coming of Jesus Christ into the world. God's promises were fulfilled in Christ.

Moses and the Jewish Law. The Israelites escaped from their slavery in Egypt, and they wandered in the desert for forty years before they entered the Promised Land. During this period, God was forming the Twelve Tribes of Israel into a nation. God made a Covenant with them at Mount Sinai, and the Ten Commandments were part of that agreement. In the course of time, many other laws were added.

The Old Testament Prophets. A prophet was a man chosen by God to be His spokesman. The aim of the prophets was to call the Israelites back to worship the one true God. The three Major Prophets are:

(1) Isaiah. At least three different people wrote the Book of Isaiah. Chapters 1-39 are prophecies in Judah (740 – 700BC). Chapters 40-55 belong to the Jewish Exile in Babylon. Chapters 56-66 are about the period after the Return from Exile and the re-building of the Temple.

(2) Jeremiah. He prophesied in Judah from 626 to 585BC when Jerusalem was captured, and the Israelites were taken into Exile in Babylon. He looked forward to a time when God would make a New Covenant with His people, which happened with the coming of Christ.

(3) Ezekiel. (592 – 570BC). This great prophet had visions, including the vision of the Valley of Dry Bones, which looks forward to the Resurrection. (Ezekiel 37.1-14)

The Writings. In the OT there are different types of writings, including legends and myths (as in the early chapters of Genesis), history, stories (e.g. Ruth, Jonah, Job, Esther and Daniel). Short pithy sayings called Proverbs, and the Psalms. Politics also have a role.

The Psalms. These hymns, poems and prayers have an important role in Jewish and Christian worship. Some are from the pen of King David, and others were written by various people over many centuries. Some are songs of praise or thanksgiving, and others are prayers for guidance, help and protection. The "Penitential Psalms" ask God for forgiveness. The Psalms are loved as they contain facts and feelings, fears, passions, anger, curses, and even a desire for revenge on our enemies. Some were written for the king. When the monarchy ended, these "Royal Psalms" were thought of in terms of the coming Messiah.

The Apocrypha. Jews living outside the Holy Land translated the Hebrew OT into Greek (about 300BC). They included 15 other spiritual writings which are called the Apocrypha. About 100AD, the Jews living in the Holy Land rejected these 15 Books. Protestant Churches do not accept the Apocrypha, whilst Roman Catholics, the Orthodox Churches and Anglicans include the Apocrypha as part of their Sacred Scriptures.

The Books of the Apocrypha are I and II Esdras, Tobit, Judith, Esther, The Wisdom of Solomon, Ecclesiasticus, Baruch, The Epistle of Jeremy, The Song of the Three Holy Children, The History of Susanna, Bel and the Dragon, The Prayer of Manasses, and I and II Maccabees.

The Apocrypha is not printed in every Bible. When buying a new one, check to see that it is included.

MAIN EVENTS IN THE NEW TESTAMENT

Scholars may disagree about the dates of some of the events in the NT.

7BC The Roman Census was taken throughout the Roman Empire to count the number of men available for military service and to pay taxes. That was probably the year when Jesus was born.

25AD Caiaphas became High Priest in Jerusalem.

26AD Pontius Pilate became Procurator (Roman Ruler) of Judaea.

27AD St John the Baptist begins his mission. He prepares for the coming of the Messiah. There is a strong national feeling, and the people want the Roman soldiers out of their country. King Herod killed John, and after that, Jesus started his public ministry.

30AD The probable date of the Crucifixion of Jesus.

36AD St Stephen stoned to death. The first Christian martyr. (Acts 7)

37AD Conversion of St Paul. Previously called Saul of Tarsus. (Acts 9)

43AD St James the Great (brother of John) is killed. King Agrippa also imprisons Peter. (Acts 12)

46 – 48AD St Paul's First Missionary Journey. (Acts 13-14)

49AD The Jews were expelled from Rome by the Emperor Claudius.

49AD The Council of Jerusalem. This decided that Gentile converts did not have to keep the Jewish Law. (Acts 15)

30 – 65AD The Oral Period. The Gospels were not written down, but passed on by word of mouth.

50 – 64AD The Sayings of Jesus. (document called "Q").

50 – 52AD St Paul's Second Missionary Journey. (Acts 15.36-18.22)

53 – 58AD St Paul's Third Missionary Journey. (Acts 18.33)

58AD St Paul returns to Jerusalem and is arrested. (Acts 21)

58 – 60AD St Paul is a prisoner at Caesarea. (Acts 24-26)

60 – 61AD St Paul's voyage to Rome. (Acts 27-28). The storm at sea, and the winter in Malta.

61 – 64AD St Paul a prisoner at Rome. – under military guard.

62AD St James (brother of Jesus) is martyred. – by stoning.

64AD The Great Fire of Rome. The Emperor Nero blames Christians and so Christians are persecuted. St Peter and St Paul probably die in this persecution. Christians were burned on Crosses.

64AD St Mark's Gospel is written at Rome. It is a widely held view that St Mark's Gospel was the first to be written. It was based on St Peter's accounts, and was written partly to encourage Christians to remain faithful during times of persecution.

66AD The Jewish Revolt against Rome begins. Jerusalem was destroyed by the Romans in 70AD. The Temple is burned, and the Jews were sent to different parts of the Empire. They finally returned when the State of Israel was created in 1948.

70AD The Christian Church was separated from Jewish worship.

64 – 313AD The Roman persecution. This was severe but spasmodic. It ended when the Emperor Constantine became a Christian in 313.

c70 – 75AD St Luke's Gospel. It was based on St Mark's Gospel and other sources. (The Acts of the Apostles c 80AD)

c80 – 85AD St Matthew's Gospel. Also based on St Mark and other sources.

c80 – 100AD St John's Gospel.

c100AD The death of St John at Ephesus.

CONTENTS OF THE NEW TESTAMENT

There are 27 books in the NT. They are divided into four main sections:–

1. THE FOUR GOSPELS. These are not "Biographies" in the modern sense, but aim to show that Jesus of Nazareth was the Son of God, who came to save mankind from their sins. The events and teaching were recorded by people who saw and heard Jesus.

St Mark's Gospel. (about 65AD). Mark was the first to write down the Gospel, about 35 years after the Resurrection. It is based on the recollections of St Peter. It is a vivid record, in a carefully arranged order. Mark is interested in supernatural events, and stresses that Jesus is the Messiah. He often uses the word "immediately". There is a "reserve" or reluctance in the Gospel to spread the news that Jesus is the Messiah. The suffering and death of Christ take up a quarter of the Gospel.

St Matthew's Gospel. (about 85 – 90AD). It was written mainly for Jews, to show that Jesus was the expected Messiah. The Christian religion is the fulfilment of the Old Testament. Jesus is the Son of David. It contains the Sermon on the Mount, and the Birth Stories (seen from the point of view of Joseph).

St Luke's Gospel. (about 80 – 85AD). Written by Luke the Physician to someone called Theophilus to show that Jesus is the Messiah. He includes the Birth Stories (from Mary's point of view). The Gospel has universal significance, and is not limited to the Jews. He brings out the compassion and concern of Jesus for the poor, the outcast and the sinner, and the role of women in society. Prayer and the work of the Holy Spirit are stressed in this Gospel.

St John's Gospel. Some believe it was written late (about 95AD) at Ephesus and others believe it was much earlier. It was probably not written by St John the Apostle, the "Beloved Disciple". It is more likely that it was written by one of his followers. There are striking differences between the first three Gospels (the Synoptic Gospels) and the Fourth Gospel. This Gospel sees the miracles as "signs". There are long speeches (discourses) usually based on the "I AM" sayings of Jesus. The other Gospels have parables and pithy sayings. St John reflects on the spiritual meaning of the death and resurrection of Jesus. He writes about Eternal Life, which Christians can start to enjoy in this world. He sees the importance of the Incarnation, when the "Word became flesh". This is the basic doctrine of Christianity.

2. THE ACTS OF THE APOSTLES. (about 85 – 90AD). St Luke continues the story from the end of his Gospel, written for Theophilus. It starts with the coming of the Holy Spirit at Pentecost. The rapid growth of the infant Church is described in vivid detail. Sometimes St Luke is travelling with St Paul (Thus he writes "we" instead of "they"). It includes the early ministry of St Peter. Then the conversion and missionary work of St Paul, up to his (final?) imprisonment in Rome (61 – 64AD).

3. THE LETTERS. There are 21 letters (Epistles) in the New Testament. St Paul wrote most of them. St Peter wrote one (II Peter also bears his name). St John wrote three (I, II and III John). There are also letters by St James, St Jude, and a long letter to the Hebrews by an unknown author.

St Paul made three great missionary journeys and he established Christian Churches in many countries around the Mediterranean. Later on, he wrote to these small and fragile Churches to encourage them and to build up their faith. He also deals with a number of specific subjects and problems in his letters.

St Paul had a brilliant brain, and some of his writings are complex and not easy to understand. The more you read them, the deeper the understanding. (e.g. Letter to the Romans). His main theme is how we are reconciled to God through the death and resurrection of Christ.

4. THE REVELATION OF ST JOHN THE DIVINE. (c 95AD). This last book of the Bible contains visions (revelations) of St John. Because of his faith, he was sent as a prisoner to the tiny island of Patmos. It is in code-like language and it encourages Christians to remain faithful during persecution. God will judge the persecutors. There is a vision of worship. Jesus is the Lamb of God who was slain and is now at the Throne of God in heaven. The Bible begins with the creation of the world. It ends with a vision of a new creation, "a new heaven and a new earth, which shall not pass away".

HOW THE BIBLE CAME INTO EXISTENCE

How were the books chosen for the Old Testament? The books of the OT were not all written at the same time. They come from a period of 1,000 years or more before the time of Christ. The Bible is a collection of sacred writings. A 'Canon' is a list of the books which are officially recognised as Sacred Scripture by the Church. A Canon guarded the truth and helped to reject false beliefs. Writings in the official Canon were used to test new writings. Did they, or did they not contain the truth?

Deciding which books to include was as a gradual process over a long period of time. The OT Canon was accepted by the Jewish Rabbis at the Council of Jamnia in 90 AD. This final list was probably settled long before this, as the books were used regularly in worship.

A sacred book was found as early as 621BC, when the Temple was repaired (2 Chronicles 34.14-22). Jesus loved and valued the Jewish Scriptures (OT), which was the only Bible existing at that time. Gathering and choosing the books for the OT was a complicated process. The Holy Spirit inspired both the writers, and those who collected the books together.

The OT (Hebrew Bible) has three main divisions: the Law, the Prophets and the Writings. **The Law** (Torah) was the first section to be recognised as Scripture. This probably happened before 300BC.

The Prophets and the Writings. Decisions about the rest of the OT took place slowly in the centuries before Christ. The Canon of the Prophets was accepted about 200BC. The Canon of the Writings was agreed about 100BC. There may well have been some over-lapping.

The Christian Church accepted the decisions made by the Jews about the Hebrew Bible. We owe a great debt of gratitude to those who chose and preserved for us the unique spiritual heritage of the Old Testament.

The Apocrypha. Jews living outside Palestine (The Dispersion) included 15 additional writings in their version of the OT, called the Apocrypha. The early Church used the Apocrypha. (But it was not accepted by the Jews of Palestine).

Development of the New Testament in the Oral Period (30-65AD).
After the Resurrection of Jesus, the Gospel was passed on by word of mouth. Jesus sent the Apostles to preach the Gospel to all nations. The Apostles were eyewitnesses to events in His life. Nothing was written down because they expected that Jesus would return quickly (The Second Coming). Scrolls were costly, and most people could not read. It was better to listen to someone who had actually been with Jesus. The Jews were good at remembering things.

The written stage (50 – 110AD). Eyewitnesses of the Resurrection started to die, and it became necessary to have written records. Events connected with the death and resurrection of Jesus were recorded, together with miracles and parables. This helped those who preached the Gospel, and those who heard it. No doubt the Apostles played a leading part in the making of the records. One of these documents is called "Q" (Quelle = source).

St Paul's Three Missionary Journeys. St Paul established Churches around the Mediterranean, and wrote letters to build up their faith. Copies of these were made and exchanged. "Circular letters" were passed on to other congregations. Each local Church built up its own collection of spiritual writings.

The Four Gospels. This was the next stage in forming the NT. (See "The Main Events in the NT" on page 17).

How were decisions made? It was a gradual process. Each local Church found out which writings were spiritually helpful, by their regular use in worship. The Holy Spirit played an important part in guiding this process.

Some Christian writings were rejected: These include the Didache, the Letter of Clement, the Gospel of St Peter, and other writings.

The completed Canon of the NT. The four Gospels and the Letters of St Paul were accepted in all the local Churches by about 130AD. St Athanasius (367AD) gives the exact list of books which are found in the modern NT. The full Canon of OT and NT was finalised at a Council in Rome in 382AD. But that was only formally agreeing with the decisions made by all the Churches long before that time.

HOW FAR CAN WE TRUST THE BIBLE?

Much depends on your answer. Some Christians believe that the whole Bible is literally true, without error or mistake. Other Christians question or reject much of the Bible. The traditional position is that the Bible is the inspired Word of God. It is the record of God's dealing with His "chosen people" and has unique authority. It is the main source of information which we have about God and Jesus Christ. It is His living Word for us today.

Did everything happen just as it is written in the Bible? There are real historical events in the Bible. The Jews are a proud race. They would not invent national disgrace, such as slavery in Egypt and Babylon. Unless the Resurrection of Christ is true, the Christian Church would not exist today. The Bible contains many records of actual events. There are also interpretations and comments about them. God speaks to us through them, just as He speaks to us through a sermon interpreting the Scripture.

There are "signs" and "symbols" in the Bible, and legends, myths and stories. These are not necessarily based on real events. They are used by the writers to teach spiritual truths. Two examples of stories are the books of Jonah and Daniel.

How accurate are the records? There is a "time gap" between the life of Jesus and writing the Gospels. Jesus did not record any of His teachings. Nobody wrote anything until 15 – 25 years after His death. How accurate were their memories after such a length of time? People at that time were good at remembering things, and some were trained to do so. The Bible undoubtedly contains deeply spiritual writings.

How accurate are the translations? Jesus spoke in Aramaic. The NT was written in Greek. So what we have is a translation. Only a very small number of the actual words of Jesus are recorded in the Bible. In addition, some original documents were lost, and we only have copies of the originals. However, the living Word of God certainly comes to us today through these copies and translations.

Facts about God are brought to us in different ways. Each book gives its own understanding of the truths about God. At first, God is seen as a fierce warrior. Slowly, the Jews came to understand His love.

Truths about God. Particular insights about God are brought to us in different ways. Each book gives its own understanding. No single writer, however inspired, can give us the whole truth. The Bible is one story, reaching a climax in Jesus Christ.

Scholars have different views about the Bible. Some Liberals want to re-write sections, and cut out offensive parts like the Cross! We cannot replace the Scriptures, especially with the transitory views of Liberals. Modern methods and skills do help in studying the Bible, but Christians are also under the authority and judgement of the Scriptures. The Bible is holy and we need to approach it with respect and awe.

2 Timothy 3.16: "All Scripture is inspired by God". Some parts are more spiritual than others. God entrusted His Word to the writers. He inspired and guided them and they used their own skills and minds to write His messages. But these writers were only human. They were writing about their own experiences of God, and they wrote to win people to faith in God.

The Bible contains the living Word of God. This Word of God is sometimes hidden by the word of man. It is inspired, sacred and holy. It is God's final revelation of Himself to the world. It contains help and wisdom for life in this world, and guidance to reach Heaven. Nothing can take the place of the Bible. The Bible is "given" to us, and we can accept it with faith. We can safely regard it as our principal source of reference, and source of spiritual nourishment.

Why do we read the Bible regularly? It is not an easy book. It has different levels of meaning. It challenges, rebukes and corrects us. It teaches us about God's will. It builds up our faith, hope and love. It deepens our understanding of God's ways. The Bible can be like a trusted friend. Through the Scriptures, we can see other people through God's eyes. When we read the Bible, the Holy Spirit inspires and challenges us, as He has done through the centuries.

The Bible has power to change people's lives. It proclaims the Word of God. When we read the Scriptures, we come close to God. We share the hopes, joys and sorrows of those who have gone before us. We can trust the Scriptures to feed our souls with the living Word of God for eternal life.

A COVENANT WITH GOD

God made a long preparation for the coming of Christ. God wants all people to be saved. He promised to send a Saviour to rescue us from our sins. To prepare the world for the coming of Christ, God chose one nation – the Israelites, or Jews. God slowly taught His chosen people about His own nature and will. They came to realise they had a special relationship with God. In the Bible, this relationship is called a Covenant, or solemn agreement. God always takes the initiative: "I will be your God, and you will be my people." No legal document was signed, sealed and delivered. That would be difficult, as God is Spirit. The benefits of the Covenant were always on the side of the people. Under the terms of the Covenant, the people were to turn away from false 'gods'. They were to follow and serve the true and living God. In return, God would help them in war. There were always conditions attached to each Covenant. Problems arose because the Israelites failed to keep their side of the agreement.

The Covenant with Noah. (Genesis 9.1-17). Like Adam and Eve, Noah is not a real person. The writer is describing God's relationship with His people through a myth or story. He punished the people for their evil ways by sending a flood. Noah and his family are saved by the Ark. (Christians are saved through the waters of Baptism by the Ark or ship of the Church). God made a Covenant with Noah, and promised never again to destroy the earth. The rainbow is a sign which reminds them of this Promise.

The Covenant with Abraham. God made Himself known to Abraham. God asked him to leave his own country and to set out for a new home in the Promised Land. Abraham did so with faith. God promised that in Abraham and his children, all the nations would be blessed. God's promises were fulfilled in Old Testament times. They were fulfilled more fully in Jesus Christ and the Christian Church. Members of three world religions – Muslims, Jews and Christians, all look back to Abraham for the beginning of their faith in God.

The Covenant with Moses. The Israelites became slaves in Egypt. God rescued them through Moses (The Exodus). God made a Covenant with them at Mount Sinai through Moses. The Ten Commandments were given to the Israelites. Under the terms of the covenant, they were to have no other 'gods' but the Lord. They were called to be a holy people. They agreed to obey God's demands. An animal was then sacrificed, and Moses threw half of the blood on the altar, and the remainder on the people. In this way, the sacred Covenant was sealed. From this time on, the people thought of themselves as belonging to God.

The Covenant at Sinai foreshadows the New Covenant made not just with the Israelites, but with all people, through the blood of Jesus on Mount Calvary. The Law given through Moses was made perfect and complete with the new law of love, given by Jesus.

The Covenant with the Exiles in Babylon. Jeremiah called for God's people to repent. They needed to have an inner conversion of the heart. He wrote to the Exiles in Babylon about a new Covenant, and sent them a message of hope: "Behold the days are coming, says the Lord, when I will make a new covenant with the House of Israel and the House of Judah … I will put my law within them, and I will write it upon their hearts; and I will be their God, and they shall be my people." (Jeremiah 31.31-33)

St John the Baptist. God's Chosen People failed to keep their side of the covenant. John the Baptist called on them to repent of their sins, in order to prepare for the coming of Christ.

The New Covenant – sealed in the Blood of Christ. Jesus Christ is the Saviour who fulfilled the promises of the Old Covenants. The Israelites failed to keep their side of the agreement, because of their sins. They tried to restore their relationship with God by offering animals in sacrifices. But Hebrews 10.4 says: "It is impossible for the blood of bulls and goats to take away sins."

Christ's blood was shed on the Cross as the one perfect sacrifice. This is the New and eternal Covenant, sealed by the blood of Christ, and offered as a self-sacrifice for our sins. At the Last Supper, Jesus said "This Cup which is poured out for you is the New Covenant in my Blood". (St Luke 22.20).

Christ is the Mediator of the New Covenant. He is both Priest and victim at the altar of the Cross. It is the perfect Covenant and through it we receive the grace of God.

DID JESUS CHRIST REALLY EXIST?

Some claim that Jesus was not a real person. He was invented by Christians to create a new religion. In reply, we can put forward many facts against this view. The Gospels could have been written as late as forty years after His death. Even so, there would still have been people living who could have disputed the truth of these writings. There is independent evidence that Christians were killed because they were followers of Jesus.

There are similarities as well as differences in detail between the four Gospels, but there is no reason to believe they were invented. And who would make up a story about the Cross? To say that Jesus never existed seems to create more problems than it solves.

Another question: If Jesus performed miracles, why are his deeds not recorded by non-Christian writers? We can say in reply – villages were isolated, and there were no modern communication systems. No outside writer between 6BC and 1,000AD wrote anything to deny or doubt the existence of Jesus.

Non-Christian Evidence about the existence of Jesus. Some writers who were not Christians did confirm that Jesus existed. They are mainly hostile to Christianity. Thus their evidence is unbiased, and can be accepted as reliable. These are the best know examples:

Josephus (about 81AD). He was a Jewish historian. He wrote about "Jesus, a wise man, for he was a doer of wonderful works, a teacher." He also wrote about the stoning to death of St James, "the brother of Jesus, the so-called Christ".

Tacitus (about 110AD). He gives us the oldest Roman record about Jesus. He wrote to the Emperor Nero about the Great Fire of Rome in 64AD, and blamed Christians for starting it. He wrote "Christ was put to death in the reign of Tiberius by the procurator Pontius Pilate".

Pliny the Younger (in 112AD). He was the Roman Governor of Bythinia (Asia Minor). The rapid spread of Christianity was causing difficulties, so he wrote to the Emperor Trajan for advice. He said – "Christians meet on a fixed day before dawn, and sing a hymn to Christ as a God".

Aeutonius (about 120AD). He was a Roman historian. He wrote about Jews who were expelled from Rome in 49AD. There was a dispute about "Chrestus", who was obviously Christ.

The Emperor Constantine. It is a widely known fact that he became a Christian in 312AD, and this had far reaching effects on the whole of the Roman Empire. No one can become a Christian without believing in the existence of Jesus Christ.

The Talmud. A collection of Jewish Laws. The authors were not well disposed towards Christians. The Talmud records – "On the eve of Passover, they hanged Jesus … because he led Israel astray".

The Koran. Jesus Christ is included in the Koran, the sacred Book of Islam. The Muslims believe that Jesus was one of the Prophets.

Cathedrals and Parish Churches. The great variety of wonderful Churches and Cathedrals have been built through the centuries because people believed and trusted in Jesus Christ. This is not real evidence that Jesus did exist, but the physical presence of so many buildings cannot be set aside lightly.

Writings about Jesus. Countless books in many languages have been written about Him. The sheer number and scholarship of these books would be incredible, unless they were based on a real person.

The New Testament. There is a remarkable collection of Parables and Sayings of Jesus in the four Gospels. They have penetrating insight and unique authority. Someone must have spoken them, and there is no reason why we should not accept them on their face value as the sayings of Jesus of Nazareth.

The enemies of Christ, as well as His disciples, carefully study the New Testament, and particularly the Gospels. Both do it for different reasons, and they would not do so unless Jesus was a real person, who still has powerful influence in the world today.

The Christian Church. There would be no Church today, unless Jesus existed. It all begins and ends with Him. Countless millions meet all around the world every Sunday to worship God, because of the existence and words and actions of Jesus. Christ.

THE "INCARNATION" – GOD MADE FLESH

Every Christmas, the Church celebrates the fact that God became man in Jesus Christ. This is called the Incarnation – God taking human flesh. St John said – "the Word became flesh" in Jesus Christ. The Incarnation is starkly simple, and yet it is the foundation of all Christian belief. Christmas presents us with God as a baby lying in the manger. We can imagine the baby in the manger, but we need the "eye of faith" to see the glory of God in that baby. God and human nature came together in one person at that one place and time of human history. The birth of Jesus is the beginning of a new era in God's plan of salvation.

God is pure Spirit. At the appropriate time, God took our human flesh in the womb of His mother Mary. The body of Jesus was formed of the substance of Mary. His soul was created by God.

The idea of God becoming man is difficult. In fact, it is impossible for the human mind to understand the full meaning. It is a mystery of God. We accept this mystery by faith, rather than by reason. We cannot give any proof for our belief. Thus we see the importance of getting to know Jesus, by our prayers and reading the Bible every day. In due course, the beliefs of the Church will make more sense.

Jesus Christ was not God in disguise as a man. He was not a super man. He was an ordinary human being. He became truly man, while remaining truly God. He had two natures – one Divine and one human. God's plan of eternal salvation is based on God taking flesh in this way. The clue to the meaning of all life is found in that stable at Bethlehem.

In His great love for the human race, God came among us in the person of the Infant Christ. This was not a natural act, but a supernatural act of God. The Church does believe in the supernatural. Christmas is all about the mystery of God's love for us in Jesus Christ.

The Incarnation is the self-giving of God in love and humility. The Second Person of the eternal Trinity became a helpless baby. He became completely dependent on Mary and Joseph in His infant years. He did this as part of God's plan to rescue us from the effects of our sins.

Philippians 2.5-8: "Jesus Christ, though He was in the form of God, did not count equality with God a thing to be grasped, but emptied Himself, taking the form of a servant, being born in the likeness of men. And being found in human form, He humbled Himself and became obedient unto death, even death on a Cross."

The Nicene Creed. This gives a long description of the Incarnation in order to guard against false beliefs about the Son of God: – "I believe in one Lord Jesus Christ, the only begotten Son of God, begotten of His Father before all worlds, God of God, Light of Light, very God of very God, begotten not made, being of one substance with the Father, by whom all things were made; who for us men and for our salvation came down from Heaven, and was incarnate by the Holy Spirit of the Virgin Mary, and was made man."

Why did God take flesh in Jesus? To save us from our sins. The human race had fallen away from God. Sin separates us from God. He acted in this way to save us from the consequences of our sins.

God took our human flesh in Jesus Christ simply because He loves us, with an everlasting love. He wants us to be able to respond freely to His love for us in Jesus Christ.

Christmas Carols. Many of the well known carols are about the Doctrine of the Incarnation. Here is one verse from "Hark the herald angels sing" by Charles Wesley (1707-88):

> Christ, by highest heaven adorned, Christ the everlasting Lord,
> Late in time behold Him come, Offspring of a Virgin's womb.
> Veiled in flesh the Godhead see, Hail the incarnate Deity,
> Pleased as Man, with man to dwell, Jesus our Emmanuel.

"Christians Awake" by John Byrom (1691-1763) is another example:

> Christians awake! salute the happy morn
> Whereon the Saviour of the world was born.
> Rise to adore the mystery of love
> which hosts of angels chanted from above.
> With them the joyful tidings first began
> of God incarnate and the Virgin's Son.

THE VIRGIN BIRTH

The traditional view: The Virgin Birth (or more accurately, virgin conception) is a miracle. In other words, Jesus Christ was conceived in the womb of Mary by the power of the Holy Spirit, and without the involvement of any human father.

Reasons why some people reject – or doubt – the Virgin Birth:
Doubts have been raised during the 19th and 20th centuries for the following reasons:

1.   The Virgin Birth is a miracle. Some Christians seem to reject the whole idea of miracles.

2.   Some believe the Virgin Birth is only a "legend". They say it was invented to hide a scandal about the birth of Christ.

3.   Apart from St Matthew and St Luke's Gospels, there is no other mention of the Virgin Birth in the whole of the New Testament.

4.   It would be more in keeping with the true humanity of Jesus Christ if His conception were like that of other human beings.

5.   Some reject the Prophesy of Isaiah 7.14: "Behold, a young woman shall conceive and bear a son, and shall call his name Emmanuel." Some say that Isaiah is speaking about a young woman who lived at that time, and that it is not about the birth of the future Messiah.

6.   St Matthew traces the ancestry of Jesus through Joseph and King David back to Abraham. If Mary was "found to be with child by the Holy Spirit," why did St Matthew include this list of His ancestors? The one contradicts the other.

7.   There are some references to Jesus as the "son of Joseph". St John 1.45: "We have found Him of whom Moses in the Law, and the Prophets wrote, Jesus of Nazareth, the son of Joseph". St John 6.42: "Is not this Jesus, the son of Joseph?"

Reasons for believing in the Virgin Birth.   Clear evidence is provided in the Gospels of St Matthew and St Luke for the Virgin Birth. They both record that Jesus was conceived by the Holy Spirit.

1. Neither Joseph nor any other man was responsible for the conception of Jesus. St Matthew 1.20: "An angel of the Lord appeared to him in a dream, saying, "Joseph, son of David, do not fear to take Mary your wife, for that which is conceived in her is of the Holy Spirit."

2. St Luke 1.30-32: The angel Gabriel said, "You will conceive in your womb and bear a son ... Mary said, "How can this be, since I have no husband?" The angel said, "The Holy Spirit will come upon you, and the power of the Most High will overshadow you. The child to be born will be called holy, the Son of God."

3. The Virgin Birth fulfils the prophesy in Isaiah 7.14: "Behold, a virgin shall conceive and bear a son."

4. Under the guidance of the Holy Spirit, the Virgin Birth was included in two of the four Gospels. St Ignatius (died 107) wrote to the Church at Smyrna – Jesus is "Son of God by divine will, truly born of a virgin." Other writers show that the Virgin Birth was widely accepted in the second century. The Virgin Birth is included in the Apostles and Nicene Creed.

5. Jesus Christ brought with Him a new beginning for the human race. The Virgin Birth is one of the signs of this new beginning.

6. The Virgin Birth shows that God is the Father of Jesus. It also shows that God took human flesh in the womb of Mary. Thus it is an important event which shows the true nature of Christ – that He is both God and man.

The first Christians expected Christ to return again fairly soon (The Second Coming). When this did not happen and eyewitnesses were dying, Mary decided to share with others the wonderful news of how Jesus was conceived by the Holy Spirit.

THE BLESSED VIRGIN MARY

A special place is given to Mary by all Christians, because she was chosen to be the Mother of God's Son. Christians differ on whether it is right to pray to Mary. However, a better understanding of Mary can deepen our faith and spiritual life.

The Early Church called Mary "The Second Eve". The first Eve was tempted by the Serpent in the Garden of Eden to rebel against God. The Second Eve, Mary, responded with faith to God's special calling.

The Annunciation. God's promises were being fulfilled when the Angel Gabriel said to Mary – "You will conceive and bear a Son, and you shall call His name Jesus". Mary had doubts, but she gave her consent – "I am the handmaid of the Lord. Let it be to me according to your Word." (St Luke 1.36). This started her journey of faith in God's loving purposes, and she consecrated her life to God. She is an example for us to follow.

Jesus was conceived by the power of the Holy Spirit. The Church has believed from very early times that Jesus was conceived by the power of the Holy Spirit in the womb of Mary (See pages 30-31). She co-operated with the will of God, and allowed God to take human flesh in her womb, to become Man in Jesus. The human body of Jesus was formed from the flesh of Mary.

The Visitation (visit) of Mary to her cousin Elizabeth. Elizabeth recognised that her cousin Mary was special and acknowledged the unborn baby as her Lord. She said – "Blessed are you among women, and blessed is the fruit of your womb." "Why is this granted to me that the mother of my Lord should come to me?" (St Luke 1.42-3)

The Birth of Jesus. Mary gave birth to the Saviour of the world in a humble stable. The eternal Word was united to our humanity in the womb of Mary. He was "God from God, Light from Light, true God from true God."

The Mother of God. Nestorian heretics said that a baby could not be called God. The Council of Ephesus in 341AD decided that that baby was God. The Divine and the human nature are united in the Person of Christ. Thus Mary was called "Mother of God".

Presentation in the Temple. Forty days after His birth, Jesus was presented to God in the Temple. Candlemas is celebrated on 2nd February. The old Jewish Priest, Simeon, recognised the infant Jesus as the Messiah.

Mary is called Mother of the Church. At the Presentation, Simeon said to Mary: "This child is destined to be a sign that is rejected, and a sword will pierce your own soul too, so that the secret thoughts of many will be laid bare." This was fulfilled when Mary saw her Son dying on the Cross. 'Jesus said to His mother, "Woman, behold your Son!" Then He said to the Beloved Disciple, "Behold your mother!" And from that hour, the disciple took her to his own home.' (St John 19.27). Thus, Jesus gave His Mother to the Church, through the Beloved disciple St John. So Mary is called Mother of the Church.

Mary at Pentecost. Mary was with the Apostles at the beginning of the Church in the Upper Room. The Holy Spirit came on them like "tongues of fire". Just as Mary co-operated with the Holy Spirit in the birth of the Messiah, so she is here praying at the birth of the Church.

The Assumption. The death of Mary is called "The falling asleep" or "Dormition". It is widely believed that when Mary died, she did not have to wait for the general resurrection of the dead. She was taken up at once, body and soul, into the glory of Heaven. She followed in the footsteps of Our Lord all through His earthly life. She gained her crown of righteousness. She left this life to be forever with her Son in Heaven. The Feast of the Assumption is celebrated in Roman Catholic and Anglican Churches on 15th August.

Mary and Prayer. Just as we ask a friend to pray for us, so we can ask Mary to pray for us. She is part of the praying community of Heaven. We link our prayers with her constant prayers. But we must always remember that Jesus Christ is the only mediator between us and God. Mary was affected by the death and resurrection of Jesus, just like any other Saint or Christian. But Mary is very close to her risen and glorified Son. Through the centuries, Christians have honoured Mary as their spiritual Mother. Thousands upon thousands make pilgrimages, year after year, to Walsingham (Norfolk), Fatima (Portugal) and Lourdes (France) to pray at these and other Shrines of Mary. We do well to honour Mary, and to ask for her prayers.

JESUS CHRIST – WAS HE GOD OR MAN?

Was Jesus Christ a human being – or was he God? It took the Early Church over 400 years to produce an answer. We begin with the NT.

1. Jesus Christ was a human being. The evidence of the Gospels is clear. Jesus of Nazareth was a complete human being in every sense. He had an ordinary human body, and he was born of a human mother. He was circumcised on the eighth day, like other Jewish boys. He developed and grew in knowledge, and in a physical way. He had normal human feelings. He felt hunger and thirst. He grew tired. He was angry. He felt compassion for the crowds. He prayed to God. He wept when Lazarus died. He was put to death by his enemies, and was buried in a new tomb. Jesus was fully human in every way – with one exception. He was without sin. But if Jesus Christ were just an ordinary man like ourselves, then that would be the end of the story.

2. Jesus Christ was God. The first disciples soon realised that Jesus was more than just an ordinary man. Jesus healed the sick and he performed miracles. He taught with authority. He was raised from the dead on the third day. Here are texts to support the "Divinity" of Jesus Christ:

St John 1.1 and 14. "In the beginning was the Word, and the Word was with God, and the Word was God ... And the Word became flesh and dwelt among us, full of grace and truth."
St Mark 14.61-2. The High Priest asked, "Are you the Christ, the Son of the Blessed?" Jesus said, "I am; and you will see the Son of Man sitting at the right hand of power, and coming with the clouds of Heaven."
St Luke 8.28. A man who had demons said, "What have you to do with me, Jesus, Son of the Most High God?"
St John 10.30. Jesus said, "I and my Father are one."
St John 19.7. The crowds answered "We have a Law that says he ought to die, because he claimed to be the Son of God."
Hebrews 1.1-3. In many and various ways God spoke of old to our fathers by the prophets; but in these last days He has spoken to us by a Son ... He reflects the glory of God and bears the very stamp of His nature, upholding the universe by His Word of power.
(See also St Matthew 14.33; 16.27; 27.43 St Mark 16.16; St Luke 10.22; St John 1.1-14; 3.35-6; 5.25; 6.40 and 10.36; Hebrews Chap 1)

The Early Church came to believe that Jesus Christ is both God and a human being. How did they come to this view? To find an answer, we look step by step at the decisions made by the Church. The Holy Spirit clearly guided the Early Church in dealing with these problems.

The first heresy (Docetism) said that Jesus was not fully human. He only seemed to be human. This heresy is corrected by St John's Gospel: "The Word (Jesus Christ) became flesh and dwelt among us." (St John 1.14). Belief in the humanity of Jesus became a test of true faith: "Every spirit which confesses that Jesus Christ has come in the flesh is of God." (1 John 4.2)

The Seven "General Councils" of the Church. These were held before the Church divided into East and West in 1063AD. Decisions of the united Church are accepted by all branches of the Church.

First Council at Nicaea in 325AD. The second heresy (Arianism – taught by a priest called Arius) stated that Jesus Christ was not God – but was "created" by God the Father. The Council rejected this, and decided that Jesus Christ is "God from God, light from light, true God from true God; begotten, not made, being of one substance with the Father". (part of the Nicene Creed, still used at the Eucharist today).

Second Council at Constantinople in 381AD. The First Council stressed that Christ was God. This Council decided that Jesus was fully human, with a human soul. (It condemned "the Apollinarian heresy," which said that there was no complete manhood in Christ).

Third Council at Ephesus in 431AD. The Church had decided that Jesus Christ was both God and man. This Council upheld the unity of Christ. There is only one Person in Christ. (This Council condemned the "Nestorian heresy" that Christ is two Persons). The title "The Mother of God" was confirmed for the Blessed Virgin Mary.

Fourth Council at Chalcedon (Turkey) in 451AD. This produced the classic statement – "One Person with Two Natures" in Jesus Christ. He did not cease to be God when He became Man. There is an "abiding union" between Godhead and Manhood in Jesus Christ. This is the official position (perhaps not the final answer but it does lay down limits for orthodox belief).

THE DIFFERENT NAMES USED FOR JESUS

Much can be learned by looking at the different names which the Church uses to describe Jesus:

The name of Jesus. Jesus is the Greek form of Joshua, and it means "God saves". He was given that name by the Angel Gabriel at the Annunciation, "Behold, you will conceive in your womb and bear a son, and you shall call his name Jesus." (St Luke 1.31). St Peter said "And there is salvation in no one else, for there is no other name under heaven given among men by which we must be saved." (Acts 4.12)

The Lamb of God. John the Baptist said of Jesus "Behold, the Lamb of God, who takes away the sin of the world". (St John 1.29). The Jewish High Priest sacrificed a Lamb at the Passover Festival. Jesus offered himself on the Cross as the Passover Lamb (Paschal Lamb).

The Son of David. The Jews looked back to the golden age of King David. God had promised to send a Messiah or Saviour, who would be the Son of David. Jesus asked "What do you think of the Christ? Whose son is he?" They said "The son of David". (St Matthew 22.42).

The Carpenter of Nazareth. Jesus worked in his father's business.

The New Adam. In the Genesis stories (myths), the first "Adam" fails because he disobeys God. Christ is the New Adam, who is "obedient unto death, even death on a Cross." (Philippians 2.8).
"The first man was from the earth, a man of dust; the second man is from heaven." (1 Corinthians 15.45).

The Rabbi. The Jews thought of Jesus as a Rabbi or Teacher. "The crowds were astonished at his teaching, for he taught as one who had authority, and not as one of the Scribes." (St Matthew 7.28-9).

Christ. It is a Greek word, meaning "Anointed One". It is a translation of the Hebrew word for the Messiah. "You are the Christ, the Son of the living God." (St Matthew 16.16).

Servant. This was to fulfil what was spoken by the prophet Isaiah: "Behold, my servant, whom I have chosen". (St Matthew 12.17).

Jesus is Lord. A leper said to Jesus: "Lord, if you will, you can make me clean". (St Matthew 8.2).

The Son of God. Those in the boat worshipped Him, saying, "Truly you are the Son of God". (St Matthew 14.33)

Son of Mary. Jesus had a human mother, and He was a complete human being.

Emmanuel. "A young woman shall conceive and bear a son, and shall call his name Emmanuel", (meaning "God with us"). (Isaiah 7.14).

Teacher. "Teacher, we saw a man casting out demons" (St Mark 9.38).

The Son of Man. Jesus chose this title, because it was not connected with the popular Jewish hope for a military Saviour. "I saw in the night visions, and behold, with the clouds of heaven there came one like a son of man." (Daniel 7.13).

The Word of God. "And the Word became flesh and dwelt among us, full of grace and truth." (St John 1.14).

Jesus as King. Pilate said "So you are a king?" Jesus answered, "You say that I am a king. For this I was born, and for this I have come into the world, to bear witness to the truth." (St John 18.37)

Jesus was God. St Thomas said to Jesus: "My Lord and my God". (St John 20.28).

Jesus the Prince of Peace. We find our peace through forgiveness and reconciliation with God, and with each other.

Jesus the Alpha and the Omega. "I am the Alpha and the Omega, the first and the last, the beginning and the end." (Revelation 22.13).

The "I am" sayings of Jesus. "I am the bread of life" (S John 13.1). "I am the light of the world" (St John 8.12). "I am the door of the sheep" (St John 10.7). "I am the Good Shepherd" (St John 10.11). "I am the resurrection and the life" (St John 11.25). "I am the way, the truth and the life" (St John 14.6). "I am the true vine" (St John 15.1)

37

EVENTS IN THE LIFE OF JESUS

It is not possible to write a complete "Life of Jesus" from the Gospel records. Nevertheless we do know about important events in His life:

The Birth of Jesus. His Birth is recorded both in St Matthew's and St Luke's Gospel. He was born in Bethlehem about 7BC, because Joseph and Mary were there for the Roman Census. Later, they fled to Egypt to escape King Herod's persecution. After Herod's death, they were able to return to Nazareth.

The Hidden Years. As far as we know, Jesus had a normal childhood with His Mother Mary and step-father Joseph. He worked in the family carpentry business. Little is known of these "hidden years," apart from a pilgrimage to the Temple when he was twelve years old. St Luke 2.48: "Did you not know I must be in my Father's house."

Baptism and Temptation. When Jesus was about 30 years old, He was baptised in the River Jordan by St John the Baptist, His second cousin. This was a powerful spiritual experience. It confirmed for Jesus that He was the Son of God, and that He was being called by God for His special ministry. His Baptism was the beginning of His public ministry. It was followed by Forty Days of Temptation in the desert, when He reflected on His vocation and how it was to be fulfilled.

The Kingdom of God. Jesus is the greatest teacher that the world has ever known. The main subject of His teaching was the Kingdom of God. In fact, the Kingdom was fulfilled in Jesus Himself. His Kingdom is present when men and women accept God as King in their lives.

The work and mission of Jesus. Most people misunderstood the nature of His mission. They hoped for a Messiah who would lead a rebellion. They wanted the hated Roman Rulers to be thrown out of their country. Instead of this, Jesus came to establish a Kingdom of justice and love and truth.

The Twelve Apostles. After a night of prayer, Jesus carefully chose twelve men to be His Apostles. In addition to His teaching in public, Jesus also trained the Twelve in private, so that they could continue His work after He had left them at the Ascension.

Opposition to Jesus. He was popular with the people. He taught with authority. But the Jewish leaders were jealous, and they were openly trying to kill Him. He became more and more aware of His coming death.

The Transfiguration. Jesus shared this strange visionary experience on the mountain with Peter, James and John. For the disciples, it confirmed that Jesus was the Messiah. For Jesus, it confirmed that the way of the Cross was what God wanted for Him. (St Luke 9.28-36).

The Last Week. Jesus made His Triumphal Entry into Jerusalem. Four days later, He kept the Passover Festival with the Twelve in the Upper Room. During that Last Supper, Jesus instituted the Sacrament of Holy Communion. Afterwards, He waited in the Garden of Gethsemane to be arrested by the Temple Guards.

The Three Trials of Jesus. Two secret trials were held during the night, one before Annas (the former High Priest), and another before Caiaphas (the present High Priest). In the morning, a third trial was held before the Roman Governor Pontius Pilate. The Jewish leaders asked for the death sentence. Pilate found Jesus was innocent, but eventually gave in to their demands.

Death on a Cross. Jesus had a long and terribly painful death on the Cross. He was buried in a new grave belonging to Joseph of Arimathaea. The disciples were utterly dejected. They thought all their hopes and plans had been destroyed by His death.

Resurrection on the third day. The disciples did not expect Jesus to rise from the dead. He first showed Himself to Mary of Magdala, and then to disciples in different "appearances" during the "Great Forty Days". His purpose was to convince them that he was risen indeed from the dead. He then commissioned the Twelve to be His Apostles, and they became the foundation pillars of His new Church.

The Ascension and Pentecost. Jesus returned to His place in the Godhead (Heaven). The Ascension was His farewell to His Apostles. He promised to be with them always "even to the end of time". He fulfilled His promise by sending the Holy Spirit at Pentecost (Whitsun). The Spirit came on their heads "like tongues of fire".

THE SEVEN LAST "WORDS" FROM THE CROSS

The last words of a dying person tell us a great deal about that person. The Seven Last Words – or sentences – of Jesus on the Cross are really like an opening into the very heart of God. What do the last words of Jesus Christ really mean? Only when we reflect on their meaning will they begin to reveal the true nature of their riches. They are worth returning to, again and again, throughout life.

1. "Father, forgive them, for they know not what they do." (St Luke 23.33). The Roman soldiers were only doing their job. Jesus forgave them because He loved them – despite their ignorance and actions. Such is the generosity of God's forgiveness. He removed the burden of guilt from the soldiers.

When we are truly sorry for our sins and turn to God, He will forgive us. His forgiveness will bring us closer to Him, and give us His peace.

2. "Today, you will be with me in Paradise." (St Luke 23.43). The Penitent Thief said – "Jesus, remember me when you come in your Kingly power." He turned to Christ at the very hour of his death. He was not rescued from that terrible agony of dying on the Cross, but he was given inner peace. Jesus made him a promise, and he trusted in that promise.

We may not know when our last hour on earth will be, but we can trust in His promises. We can pray with Mary – "Holy Mary, Mother of God, pray for us sinners, now, and at the hour of our death. Amen."

3. "Woman, behold your Son!" Then he said to the disciple, "Behold, your mother!" (St John 19.27). Mary stood at the foot of the Cross, and watched the life of her Son drain away in agony. Joseph had died some time ago, so Jesus entrusted His Mother to the care of St John, the Beloved Disciple. "Behold, your mother." In due course, she went with St John to Ephesus.

The death of Jesus was a critical stage in the formation of the Church. It was the very moment when our redemption was being won for us on the Cross. Many people regard this as the time when Mary became not only the Mother of the Beloved Disciple – but also the Mother of all Christians – the Mother of the Church.

4. **"My God, my God, why hast Thou forsaken me?"** (St Mark 15.34). These words are profound and awe inspiring. Pain and suffering were partly responsible for Jesus crying out. Jesus alone knew the agony of separation from God, because only He knew the joy of perfect union with God. He felt forsaken because He was bearing the sins of the whole world, past, present and future. That was an incredible – an unimaginable burden to bear.

If we feel the dark pain of being forsaken by God, we can remember the words of St Paul – "Nothing can separate us from the love of God in Christ Jesus." Jesus said – "I am with you always." We can turn to God in prayer with these words of Jesus.

5. **"I thirst."** (St John 19.28). After hanging in the heat on the Cross, suffering terrible pain both in body and spirit, Jesus cried out – "I thirst." This thirst was much greater than a desire for a drink. His thirst was a thirst for the souls of men and women everywhere in every age. It includes those who respond to His love, and those who reject Him. "I thirst" speaks to us of the mystery of the love of God for us all, and His desire for us to respond to that love.

6. **"It is finished."** (St John 19.30). Jesus is not so much thinking of the end of His suffering on the Cross. He is really speaking about the completion of God's work, which He set out to do. His one perfect sacrifice of Himself on the Cross is finished. Jesus endured the suffering and pain and torture, and so He won that great victory on the Cross. This sixth Word is a cry of triumph – "It is finished."

God has touched our lives, and He wants to guide us and lead us in His ways of justice and peace. He wants us to remain faithful unto death, and to complete the work which he has for each of us to do.

7. **"Father, into Thy hands I commit my spirit."** (St Luke 23.46). All is now over, and the last thing He does is to commend His spirit to His Heavenly Father. Countless Christians use this prayer, before sleep, when in great pain, or as they draw near to death.

To whom else could we commit our spirit – other than to God? He is the giver of life – and after our earthly journey is over, we give our life back to God. Jesus is the Way, the Truth and the Life.

THE DEATH OF JESUS IN THE BIBLE

Jesus was crucified when Pontius Pilate was Roman Governor of Judaea. What is the meaning of His death? The Cross stands at the centre of every Eucharist. We find eternal life through the self-offering of Jesus. It is important for Christians to think deeply about His death. Thus we look at this through some of the writers in the Bible:

THE BOOK OF GENESIS.
Genesis 22.7-8. Isaac said, "Behold the fire and the wood; but where is the lamb for a burnt offering?" Abraham said, "God will provide Himself the lamb for the burnt offering."

THE PROPHET ISAIAH.
There are four "Songs of the Suffering Servant" in the Book of Isaiah. About 600 years later, Jesus identified Himself with this Suffering Servant. Perhaps he learned it by heart, and thought of His mission in these terms.

Isaiah, chapter 53 – He was despised and rejected by men;
a man of sorrows and acquainted with grief.
Surely he has borne our griefs and carried our sorrows;
yet we esteemed him stricken, smitten by God, and afflicted.
But he was wounded for our transgressions,
he was bruised for our iniquities;
upon him was the chastisement that makes us whole,
and with his stripes we are healed.
All we like sheep have gone astray;
we have turned everyone to his own way.
And the Lord has laid on him the iniquity of us all.
He was oppressed and he was afflicted, yet he opened not his mouth.
Like a lamb that is led to the slaughter
and like a sheep that before its shearers is dumb,
so he opened not his mouth.
And he made his grave with the wicked
and with a rich man in his death, although he had done no violence,
and there was no deceit in his mouth.
Yet it was the will of the Lord to bruise him;
he was put to grief when he makes himself an offering for sin.

SAINT PAUL.
Romans 5.8 – God shows His love for us in that while we were yet sinners, Christ died for us.

Philippians 2.8 – Christ "being found in human form, humbled Himself and became obedient unto death, even death on a Cross.
1 Cor 6.20 – You are not your own. You were bought with a price.

SAINT PETER. He may have been present when Jesus was nailed to the Cross. He wrote to encourage Christians during fierce persecution.
1 Peter 3.18 – Christ died for sins once for all, the righteous for the unrighteous, that He might bring us to God.
1 Peter 2.20 – If when you do right and suffer for it you take it patiently, you have God's approval.
1 Peter 4.13 – Rejoice in so far as you share Christ's sufferings, that you may also rejoice and be glad when His glory is revealed.

SAINT MATTHEW.
St Matthew 26.2 – Jesus said "You know that after two days the Passover is coming, and the Son of Man will be delivered up to be crucified."

SAINT MARK.
St Mark 10.33-4 – Jesus said "Behold, we are going up to Jerusalem, and the Son of Man will be delivered to the chief priests and the scribes, and they will condemn Him to death, and deliver Him to the Gentiles, and they will mock Him, and spit upon Him, and scourge Him, and kill Him; and after three days He will rise again.
St Mark 14.24 – Jesus said "This is my blood of the Covenant, which is poured out for many."

SAINT LUKE.
St Luke 22.42 – "Father, if Thou art willing, remove this cup (of suffering) from me. Nevertheless, not my will, but Thine be done."

SAINT JOHN. He sees the crucifixion as the "Coronation" of Christ.
St John 18.27 – Jesus replied (to Pilate) "You say that I am a King. For this I was born, and for this I have come into the world, to bear witness to the truth."
St John 12.23 – The hour has come for the Son of Man to be glorified.
St John 12.24 – Unless a grain of wheat falls into the earth and dies, it remains alone. But if it dies, it bears much fruit.
St John 12.32 – And I, when I am lifted up from the earth, will draw all men to myself.

WHY DID JESUS DIE ON THE CROSS?

A reply from the Jewish point of view. The words and actions of Jesus gave a clear message about the love and forgiveness of God. His teaching was different from that of the Jewish Leaders. In fact, Jesus was a threat to the established religion of the day. So Jesus had to die.

A reply from the point of view of the Romans. The Roman Empire wanted law, order and stability above all else. Pontius Pilate eventually gave in to the demand for the death penalty made by the Jewish leaders. St Luke 23.2: "We found this man perverting our nation, and forbidding us to give tribute to Caesar, and saying that He Himself is a King."

A reply from the point of view of the Christian Church. A simple answer is: Jesus died to save us from our sins. The meaning of this has not been formally discussed at a Council of the Church (as happened with the "meaning" of Jesus Christ and the Holy Trinity).

What did Jesus think about His death? Here are three answers:
(1) The Prophet Isaiah spoke about a Suffering Servant. Isaiah 53.4: "Surely he has borne our griefs and carried our sorrows" Jesus probably saw His work in terms of this Suffering Servant. He predicted His death, and told His disciples that He would be put to death, and rise again on the third day.
(2) When the 10 Commandments were given, Moses sprinkled the blood of an animal on the people to seal the Covenant between God and the Jews. Centuries later, Jesus thought of His own blood as sealing the New Covenant. St Mark 14.24: "This is my Blood of the Covenant, which is poured out for many."
(3) Jesus died to save us from our sins. He did not have to die on the Cross. He was not caught off guard by the Temple Police. He chose to die, because He knew the Cross was part of God's plan for our salvation. In the Garden of Gethsemane before His arrest, Jesus prayed that the cup (of suffering or destiny) might pass from Him. Then He accepted it. St Mark 14.36: "Not my will, but your will be done."

Why did Jesus have to die? Surely God could forgive our sins without the death of Jesus? We cannot fully understand the mind of God. All we can say in this world is that it is a mystery of our faith.

44

Theories about the death of Jesus. Different answers have been given over the centuries. There is no correct answer, but each one adds to our understanding.

Jesus died as a sacrifice for our sins. The Jews sacrificed animals to take away their sins. But sin is a serious problem, from which only God can save. Thus Jesus offered Himself as a once for all sacrifice on the "Altar of the Cross". A sacrifice is a costly gift offered to God. It has to be all or nothing. The offering of one's life is the supreme sacrifice.

A lamb was sacrificed at the Passover. At the Last Supper (a Passover meal) Jesus took some bread, and He said, "This is my Body". Instead of the Lamb, He offered Himself as the Passover victim for sacrifice on the Cross on the next day.

On the Cross, God offered to us the best that He could offer – His own Son. When we think of the unity of the Trinity, we realise that God was giving Himself to us in the death of His Son. The Eucharist is closely connected with this self-offering of Christ for our salvation.

"We have been justified" through the death of Christ. (Romans 5.1). It is like being acquitted in a court of law. God found us guilty. Then God paid the penalty for us in the death of His Son Jesus Christ.

The death of Jesus was a ransom. This was the price paid to set us free from the power of sin. St Mark 10.45: "The Son of man came … to give His life as a ransom for many." In His victory on the Cross, Christ defeated the power of sin and death.

Jesus died as our Representative. He took our sins on Himself. He alone is able to represent us before God.

Jesus is our Substitute. Jesus endured the suffering we deserve for our sins. He died the death that we deserve. 2 Corinthians 4.21: St Paul – "For our sake, He made Him to be sin who knew no sin."

Je sus died to give us a moral influence. His death shows us the full extent of God's perfect sacrificial love for us. This love attracts us, and it brings us nearer to God.

THE THREE DAYS – "THE EASTER TRIDUUM"

The last three days of Holy Week are Maundy Thursday, Good Friday and Easter Eve (Holy Saturday). They are called the Easter Triduum. What happened on these three days are not separate events, but different stages in God's plan for our salvation.

The Church makes an effort to celebrate the Easter Triduum in the best way possible. Special ceremonies and "dramatic presentations" have been developed over the centuries. The purpose is to show us the real meaning of the death and resurrection of Jesus. The Church celebrates these three days because through them we have been freed from the powers of sin and death. All ornaments, hangings and candles are removed on Holy Thursday, and returned again on Holy Saturday.

Holy (or Maundy) Thursday. Jesus celebrated the Passover which commemorates the escape of the Jews from slavery in Egypt. The Last Supper was the first Eucharist to be celebrated. In our present-day Holy Thursday service, there are seven main sections, including:

The OT Reading gives instructions for keeping the Passover (Exodus 12.1-14).
The Second Reading is St Paul's earliest account of the Last Supper in 1 Corinthians 1.23-9.
In the Gospel Reading Jesus washes the feet of the Apostles. Thus the Priest washes the feet of twelve men in the service. It is an example of humble service, which Christians are invited to follow in their daily lives.
The Eucharist is celebrated.
The Blessed Sacrament is "reserved" and taken to a place which represents the Garden of Gethsemane.
The Altar is stripped bare during the service, ready for the Good Friday celebration of Christ's sacrifice on the Cross.
A Silent Vigil is kept. Sometimes it is kept through the night. "Could you not watch one hour?"

On this night, Jesus allowed Himself to be captured by His enemies. He offered Himself as the "Paschal victim" on the "Altar" of the Cross. The Blood of the lamb was smeared on the doorposts in Egypt to save the Israelites. Christians are saved by the Blood of Christ, freely shed on the Cross for our salvation.

Good Friday. Many Churches have gone back to the traditional Good Friday service (instead of the Three Hour Service). It has six parts:
Solemn readings from Scripture and the Passion Narrative, to help us to understand and enter into the suffering and death of Christ.
Prayers are offered for the needs of all people.
A draped Wooden Cross is brought into the Church in silence. The procession stops, and three times it is partly uncovered. The invitation is sung "Behold, the wood of the Cross, whereon was hung the Saviour of the world." All reply "O come, let us worship." (NEH 516A/B)
The priest and congregation venerate the Cross. This can be done in silence by people where they sit or kneel in their pew. Others come out and bow – genuflect – reverence – or kiss the wood of the Cross, as each feels appropriate.
During the Veneration, a hymn is sung – "Faithful Cross! Above all other one and only noble Tree!" (Crux Fidelis: NEH 517).
According to ancient custom, the Eucharist is not celebrated on Good Friday. Instead, the Blessed Sacrament ('reserved' on Maundy Thursday) is brought to the Altar in silence. In acknowledging Christ's death on the Cross, Christians also share His living presence through the Blessed Sacrament.

Holy Saturday Vigil. There is a rich wealth of drama in the service on Easter Eve. The service usually has five main parts:
The Service of Light. There are no lights in Church. A fire is sometimes lit outside. The "new fire" is blessed and used to light the Easter (Paschal) Candle. Five grains of incense (representing the five wounds of Christ) are inserted in the candle. The priest carries it into Church and sings "Christ our Light". All reply: "Thanks be to God". This is repeated twice inside the Church. The candles of the congregation are lit from the Easter Candle.
The Easter Proclamation – The Exsultet – is sung by the priest (or a cantor) – in praise of Christ our Light.
The Vigil Readings. These trace the acts of God in His work of salvation in former years.
The Blessing of the Water at the Font. (Sometimes adults are baptised and confirmed). All present renew their Baptismal Vows.
The First Eucharist of Easter. This is a joyful celebration, a fresh start.

THE RESURRECTION OF JESUS

God raised Jesus on the third day by the power of the Holy Spirit. There could be no Christian Church, no forgiveness of sins and no eternal life, unless Jesus had been raised from the dead. So let us look at each "objection" carefully:

Jesus did not actually die on the Cross. He only fainted or seemed to die, and recovered later in the tomb. But Jesus in fact died quickly. Pilate asked for a report from the soldier in command (St Mark 15.44-45). A soldier plunged his spear into the side of Jesus, and out came water and blood. (St John 19.30) The Fourth Gospel is also quite clear that Jesus really was dead: "but when they came to Jesus and saw that He was already dead, they did not break His legs." (St John 19.32).

Someone else was crucified. This theory is in the Koran (Muslim Sacred Scriptures written about 600AD?). But if someone else had been crucified, the Jewish Leaders, the soldiers and the crowds would all have know. The disciples and His mother would not stay there if someone had been crucified by mistake or deceit. No one would invent the "Seven Last Words of Jesus" in that form. They have a ring of truth.

The tomb was found empty because Jesus was not buried there. Jews who were crucified were usually buried in a common grave. But Joseph of Arimathaea asked Pilate for the body of Jesus. There could be no mistake about the grave which belonged to Joseph.

The Jewish Leaders removed the body. Why would they do this? They asked for a guard to be placed on the tomb in case the disciples stole the body. (St Matthew 27.62-4). If the Jewish Leaders removed the body, they only had to produce it to end all talk of rising from the dead.

The disciples removed the body. This was invented by the Chief Priests to prove that the resurrection was not true. But the Chief Priests asked for a guard at the tomb to prevent this from happening. The disciples would not steal the body, in order to pretend that Jesus had risen from the dead. They were in fact terrified for their own lives. The Risen Christ gave them courage and strength to continue His work.

The Gospel records do not agree in details. This is strong evidence that the Resurrection was not invented. Any writer making up a story would ensure that all details agreed with each other. Christianity would not have survived so long on the basis of a made up story or a lie.

The "Empty Tomb" was invented later. But the empty tomb was widely known soon after the Resurrection. It is clearly recorded in all four Gospels. St Paul knew about it within two years or so of the Resurrection of Jesus. (1 Corinthians 15 and Galatians 1.16).

The Disciples went to the wrong tomb in the dark and found the tomb empty. But if a mistake had been made, the Jewish Leaders and the disciples would surely have continued to search for the body.

The appearances of Jesus after the Resurrection were only visions or hallucinations. But this does not take account of all the facts. There were separate reports of the appearances. The two disciples on the road to Emmaus clearly had a meeting with the Risen Christ. (St Luke 24.13-35). The appearances of Jesus after the Resurrection are, in fact, an important part of the evidence.

To sum up. The first Christians were utterly convinced that Jesus had been raised from the dead. They worked to tell other people that they had seen the Risen Lord. "The Lord is risen indeed."

At first, the disciples themselves did not believe. They were dejected and terrified, in case they too were arrested and crucified. They had – in human terms – everything to gain simply by returning to their homes and families, and hoping that they would not be arrested. But they were convinced of the presence of the Risen Christ with them.

The vicious persecutions by the Romans and the Jews failed to destroy the Church. Christians through the centuries have been convinced of the Resurrection by their personal experience of the Risen Christ. When all the evidence is taken together, it very strongly suggests that it is true – so much so that countless people have given their lives for this belief.

THE ASCENSION

Traditional view of the Ascension. Forty days after the Resurrection, Jesus led the eleven Apostles to Bethany. (Eleven because Judas had killed himself). They alone saw Jesus being carried up to Heaven. The Ascension is an important article of faith. It is found in the three Creeds, and celebrated each year as a major festival of the Church.

Doubts about the Ascension. Some people say that Heaven is not up in the sky. But how else could this be described? Simple words help to explain the mystery, and they do not disprove the Ascension. Because of this, some claim the Ascension is a story – or metaphor, or symbol. There are also two problems with the original manuscripts which they believe confirm their doubts about the Ascension:

The account in St Mark 16.19. "So the Lord Jesus, after He had spoken to them, was taken up into heaven, and sat down at the right hand of God." There is a problem. Most scholars agree that the last twelve verses of the Gospel (9-20) were not written by St Mark. They were clearly added later by an unknown hand. This addition in no way disproves the truth of the Ascension.

The account in St Luke 24.51. "While He blessed them, He parted from them, and was carried up to Heaven." The words "was carried up to Heaven" are not included in some early Western Manuscripts of St Luke's Gospel. This again does not prove that the Ascension did not happen, even if these verses were added later on.

The account in Acts 1.9-11. "As they were looking on, He was lifted up, and a cloud took Him out of their sight." The Acts of the Apostles is the continuation or "second volume" of St Luke's Gospel. In this passage, St Luke is clearly re-stating the facts of the Ascension, as recorded in St Luke 24.51 (above).

The mystery of the Ascension. After the Resurrection, Jesus had a spiritual body. The Ascension was the last of the Resurrection Appearances. It was a spiritual event, and as such, it will always be a mystery and difficult to describe in human words. Even so, the Ascension was a real event, and an important one, in God's plan for our salvation.

To God, all things are possible. He created the universe. He raised Jesus from the dead. Surely it was possible for Him to raise up the spiritual body of Jesus into a cloud.

The importance of the Ascension. It helps us to understand different aspects of our faith:

1.   The Ascension is the end of Our Lord's earthly ministry. It was the completion by Jesus of the earthly part of God's plan for our salvation.

2.   The Ascension clearly shows the disciples that there will be no more Resurrection appearances by Jesus. A definite end was needed. Without it, the disciples would have wondered when the next appearance would happen.

3.   The disciples returned to Jerusalem with joy – not sorrow. They knew they now had a Master and friend in Heaven.

4.   The Ascension proclaims Jesus as Lord and King in the glory of Heaven. He now has a new existence with God. He now reigns supreme over the whole of the universe. He is now seated in majesty "at the right hand of God." He fills the universe with His presence.

5.   Jesus sent the Holy Spirit to the Church after His Ascension to Heaven. Jesus is absent from His disciples in one sense. Because He is in Heaven, He is free from the limits of time and space. Thus He is able to be present in a more personal way with the entire Church on earth through the Spirit.

6.   Because of the Ascension, we now have a great High Priest in Heaven. The ascended Jesus is our Advocate who intercedes with the Heavenly Father on our behalf.

7.   Jesus shared in our human nature. At the Ascension, He took our humanity into Heaven. The Ascension shows us the destiny which God has planned for us. Our true homeland is in Heaven.

THE HOLY SPIRIT

The Holy Spirit is a Person. He is not just a force or power or energy. He is a Person. He shows us what is right and wrong, and He convicts us of sin (St John 16.8). He guides us and teaches us. By our sins we "grieve" the Holy Spirit (Ephesians 3.20).

The Holy Spirit is God. He has always been the Third Person of the eternal Trinity. The Spirit makes God known in the world. The Spirit is "Lord and giver of life, who proceeds from the Father and the Son" (Nicene Creed).

The Holy Spirit in the Old Testament. The work of the Holy Spirit is only slowly revealed in the OT. In the creation stories, the Spirit is seen as a wind or breath which "hovers" and "broods" over the face of the waters. God made Adam and "breathed into man's nostrils the Spirit of life" (Genesis 2.7). The Spirit of God is at work through the Prophets in the OT. They realised that He is the inspiration of our conscience and the basis of our moral life. The prophets understood that the Holy Spirit would only be given or "poured out" fully at the time of Christ.

Jesus and the Holy Spirit. St Paul described the Holy Spirit as "The Spirit of Christ". Romans 8.9: "Anyone who does not have the Spirit of Christ does not belong to Him." Jesus was conceived and "made flesh" through the power of the Holy Spirit in the womb of Mary. The Holy Spirit came upon Jesus like a dove at His baptism. As a result, Jesus knew He was called by God for His special work.

The Holy Spirit drove Jesus out into the wilderness to be tempted. He dwelt fully in Jesus, and acted with power in signs and miracles.

The Holy Spirit and the beginning of the Christian Church. Jesus promised the Apostles that He would not leave them alone. "I will send to you another Comforter, who will be with you for ever." After He ascended to Heaven, this promise was fulfilled, when the Holy Spirit was poured out on the Apostles on the Day of Pentecost. Acts 1.8: "You will receive power when the Holy Spirit has come upon you; and you shall be my witnesses in Jerusalem and in all Judaea and Samaria and to the end of the earth."

There would be no Christian Church without the active presence and work of the Holy Spirit. The Church is the Spirit-filled community.

The Holy Spirit unites Christians with Christ and thus we are united with each other. He changes the bread and wine into the Body and Blood of Christ in the Eucharist. He inspires the Church, and directs her work and mission, just as He inspired the Apostles to spread the Good News of the Gospel. The Spirit has directed the work of the Church, guarding and guiding her through the centuries.

The different Names or Titles of the Holy Spirit in the Bible. The Holy Spirit is called – The Paraclete or Comforter (Strengthener) – wind – the breath of God (St John 3.5-8) – the anointing Spirit (St Luke 4.18) – the fire of the Spirit (Acts 2.3-4) – the cloud and the light in the OT (Exodus 24.15 ff) – the seal of the Spirit (St John 6.27) – the dove (Genesis 8.8-12 and St Matthew 3.16) – the Lord and giver of life – the Spirit of truth – the Spirit of love.

The Gifts of the Spirit. St Paul writes about these gifts in 1 Corinthians 12. There are different kinds of spiritual gifts – wisdom – knowledge – faith – the power to heal – and to work miracles – prophecy – speaking and interpreting tongues.

The Fruits of the Spirit. These are listed by St Paul in his letter to the Galatians (5.20) – love – joy – peace – patience – goodness – faithfulness – gentleness – self-control.

These fruits of the Spirit are the benefits which come to us when we truly try to live a Christian life, doing the will of God.

Ourselves and the Holy Spirit. God continues the saving work of Christ through the Spirit. The Spirit is given at Baptism. We receive the "seal" of the Spirit at Confirmation. He is the gift of the Father and the Son to us. Our bodies are "temples of the Spirit". Sometimes the Spirit makes His presence known to us. Even when God seems completely absent, He is with us always. The Holy Spirit encourages, supports, and challenges us. The Spirit is gentle like a dove. He is also God's almighty power. The Spirit "points" us to Christ.

THE CHURCH

What is the Church? The Church on earth is a human organisation, because it is made up of human beings. The Church is not without sin, and needs God's forgiveness in order to grow in holiness and love. The Church is also a Divine organisation, as it was created by God.

The Church is many things. It is a sign and sacrament of the presence of God in the world. It is the community of the Baptised, and the fellowship of those who share in the Eucharist. The Church is the worshipping community, which offers prayer and praise in union with Christ's ceaseless offering to God in Heaven. It is the "Bride of Christ" and the "Ark of Salvation". The Church is the community of those who acknowledge "Jesus Christ as Lord" (Philippians 2.11). The Church's task is to comfort, challenge and give hope to people.

The local Church is a very small part of the whole. It is linked by the Bishop with the Church of the Apostles (The Apostolic Succession). Christians of earlier generations form the major unseen part of the Church. The Church on earth is united with the Holy Trinity, and she has "mystic sweet communion with those whose rest is won".

The Church is the "Body of Christ". It was created to continue His work. William Temple said: "It is the only organisation which exists for those who do not belong." It's task is to proclaim the Gospel.

The roots of the Christian Church go deep into the OT. God decided to carry out His plan of salvation through the Jews. They were (and still are) God's "chosen people". God chose Abraham (about 1800BC) to be the founder of a great nation. God made a Covenant (agreement) with the Jews, but they repeatedly failed to keep their side of the bargain. The majority were "unfaithful" and they worshipped pagan "gods". A "Faithful Remnant" remained loyal to God, and from this Faithful Remnant came the Messiah.

Jesus re-created the Jewish Church. God sent His Son to continue His work of salvation which He started long ago through the Prophets. Jesus attracted Jewish disciples by His personality and teaching. He commissioned twelve men as His Apostles (representing the Twelve Tribes of Israel). These were the "foundation stones" of the new Christian Church ("the new Israel of God").

The Church and the Kingdom of God. The Kingdom came with the coming of Jesus Christ, and it grows in the hearts of those who worship and serve Him. Jesus spent His ministry proclaiming the Good News of the Kingdom of God. The Kingdom is not the same as the Church, although they are closely connected. (See pages 124-125).
The task of the Church is to bring people into the Kingdom, and all baptised Christians are called on to share in this work.

St Peter and the Church. Jesus chose St Peter for a special task. He said: "You are Peter, and on this rock I will build my Church, and the powers of death shall not prevail against it." (St Matthew 16.18). Peter was the first Bishop of Rome. The Pope is his successor, and has an important role as (unofficial) leader and spokesman of all Christians.

The Last Supper. On the night before He died, Jesus ate the Passover Meal with the Twelve Apostles, to celebrate the escape of the Israelites from slavery. It showed the vital connection between the Eucharist and His death on the Cross. This was the first celebration of the Eucharist, and it was an important stage in the creation of the new Church.

The Cross and Resurrection. Jesus offered Himself to God on the Cross for our salvation. The foundation of the Church is closely connected with this self-offering of Jesus. But the Cross would have no value without the Resurrection. The death and Resurrection are both important stages in the formation of the Church.

The Holy Spirit and the Church. Christ's work on earth was itself perfectly completed. Before He returned to Heaven, He promised to send "another Comforter." This was fulfilled at Pentecost, when the Spirit was poured out on the Church. Pentecost is called the Birthday of the Church. The Church is the Spirit filled community.

Signs and Characteristics of the Church. The Creed describes the Church as "one, holy, catholic and apostolic". It is **"one"** because we are united to Christ by Baptism and the Holy Spirit. Although sadly and sinfully divided, unity is the will of Christ. The Church is **"holy"** because it was created by God, and its members share in His life. **"Catholic"** means whole or universal. The Church is **"Apostolic"** where it still holds to the faith of the Apostles. An Apostle is one who is "sent out" by Christ to carry on His work in the world.

THE SACRAMENTS OF THE CHURCH

A Sacrament is something sacred or holy. It is the prayers of the Church, used with certain material things and actions which we can see or touch.

A Sacrament is "an outward and visible sign". It shows that we have received "an inward and spiritual gift" from God. This special gift from God is called "grace". The Sacraments are the way in which God shares with us the benefits of Christ's work of salvation.

Jesus Christ is a Sacrament from God. God uses material things in His plan for our salvation. God took flesh and became Man in Jesus Christ. Jesus is a Sacrament of God, and He is a sign of God's love. Jesus showed us this love by His words and His actions. He laid His hands on the sick. He broke bread. He put clay on the eyes of a blind man. He put His fingers in the ears of a deaf man. He offered Himself to God on the Cross.

The Church is a Sacrament of Jesus Christ. The Church has outward and visible signs in the Bishops and Priests, and in each member of the Church. We have "outward and visible" physical bodies and we also have an "inward and spiritual" life. We are "temples of the Holy Spirit" and signs of God's love in the world.

The Sacraments of the Church. God chose to continue His work of salvation through the Sacraments of the Church. These are signs of God's love for us, and through them we meet the risen Christ. God gives us His love and strength through the sacraments.

How many Sacraments are there? Peter Lombard (1158AD) named seven Sacraments – Baptism, Confirmation, Eucharist, Penance (Confession), Anointing, Ordination and Matrimony. Seven has become the traditional number of the Sacraments. Baptism and the Eucharist are called the Sacraments of the Gospel, to distinguish them from the "five commonly called Sacraments".

The outward and visible part. Every Sacrament has an "outward and visible" part, as well as an "inward and spiritual" gift of grace. The outward and visible part is divided into two – "The Matter" eg bread and wine. "The Form" is using the correct form of words.

The inward and spiritual grace given through the Sacrament. By the power of the Holy Spirit, the materials used in the Sacrament become the channels of God's grace. God gives us His special gifts and blessings through the Sacraments of the Church.

The Minister of the Sacraments. The Minister celebrating the Sacrament is not acting on his own authority, but on the authority of the whole Church. Ordination gives the Priest authority to act in the Sacrament on behalf of the Church. The ministry of the Church is a continuation of the ministry of Christ, done in His name and authority.

When did the Seven Sacraments begin? All the Sacraments have their origin in God Himself. Jesus instituted the Eucharist at the Last Supper: "He took bread, blessed it and broke it, and gave it to them, and said, "Take, this is my Body". (St Mark 14.22). He instituted the Sacrament of Baptism before He ascended into heaven. "Go, therefore, and make disciples of all nations, baptising them in the name of the Father, and of the Son, and of the Holy Spirit." (St Matthew 28.19)

The other five Sacraments come from the Apostles, who were acting on instructions from Christ. Acts 13.1: To the Apostles Jesus "presented Himself alive after His passion by many proofs, appearing to them during forty days, and speaking of the Kingdom of God". Jesus continued to instruct the Apostles during this period.

How effective are the Sacraments? The person receiving the Sacrament must have faith in Christ and His Church. The person must also be sincere. Saint Paul wrote: "all have sinned, and all fall short of the glory of God." But it is the work of the Holy Spirit on our souls, which alone makes us worthy to draw near with faith. The effectiveness of a Sacrament does not depend on our worthiness. They work whatever our feelings or spiritual awareness. But a Sacrament will not help, unless it is received in faith. God gives us His love and strength through the Sacraments, but we need to respond to His gift.

Can we say that the Church is a Sign and a Sacrament of Heaven?
"So, Lord, at length when Sacraments shall cease,
May we be one with all Thy Church above,
One with Thy Saints in one unbroken peace,
One with Thy Saints in one unbounded love:
More blessed still, in peace and love to be
One with the Trinity in Unity.   (William Turton 1838-1938)

THE SACRAMENT OF BAPTISM

Baptism is a vital Sacrament. All the other sacraments depend on our Baptism. Jesus said, "Unless one is born of water and the Spirit, he cannot enter the Kingdom of God." (St John 3.5). There are two parts to Baptism:

"The outward and visible sign" of Baptism is water. The word Baptism means plunging. Jesus offered himself on the Cross on Good Friday and He died for our sins. He conquered sin and death, and rose again on the third day. In the waters of Baptism (blessed by the priest) we plunge to our death, and rise again to new life with Christ. By the power of the Holy Spirit, we are united with His death, our sins are forgiven and we are raised to new life with Christ.

Water is either sprinkled or poured three times over the forehead. The correct "form" of words must be used, with the Threefold name – "(Mary) I baptise you in the name of the Father, and of the Son, and of the Holy Spirit. Amen."

Anyone can baptise in an emergency, but it is normally administered by a priest or deacon, during the Eucharist. Baptism is the first step in becoming a member of the Church. It is only completed with Confirmation and the Eucharist.

"The inward and spiritual" part of Baptism is grace. We can see the water (the "matter") and we can hear the correct words (the "form"). But we cannot see the "grace" given in Baptism. Grace is the unseen spiritual gift from God. It purifies us from sin, and frees us from the consequences of sin. In Baptism, we are made children of God, and we begin our new life in Christ. The grace we are given helps us to fight against evil and to grow in the Christian Faith.

The Sign of the Cross. This is made on the forehead (usually with oil blessed by the Bishop on Maundy Thursday). That Cross on the forehead soon disappears, but the benefits we receive at Baptism can never be destroyed or removed. They are indelible in character, imprinted on our souls for the rest of our earthly lives.

What is the cost of our Baptism for God? God sent his Son Jesus Christ, who "took flesh" and died on the Cross, to save us from sin and death. Thirsty in the Eastern heat, naked and in terrible pain, Jesus died for us. God shows His great love for us in Jesus. There was no half-hearted giving. He gave his life totally for us.

Our part in Baptism. The first Christians considered Baptism to be very important, giving it much prayer and careful preparation. To be a follower of Christ meant they often faced persecution and death. Promises and Duties undertaken publicly should be taken very seriously. In other words, how do we respond to what God has done for us on the Cross? God keeps His promises, and the sacrifice of Christ on the Cross is valid for every generation. Likewise we too should try seriously to keep our promises.

The role of the Church in Baptism. It is not a private arrangement between God and the candidate (and his or her family) God unites us with Christ, through the power of the Holy Spirit in Baptism. There is an unseen spiritual link between Christ, and all Christians are united with each other through their union with Christ. For this reason, Baptism is normally celebrated when the whole Church is gathered together for the main Sunday Eucharist. The congregation can then welcome the new Christian into its membership.

A new Christian can only live and grow in the Faith through the spiritual help which God provides through His Church. This help comes to the newly baptised particularly through the life and worship of the local Church. Children are baptised "on the understanding that they will be brought up as Christians within the family of the Church". Parents and Godparents promise that they will help them and encourage them by their prayers, their example and their teaching.

Baptism and Faith. When someone asks for Baptism for themselves or for a child, they need to have faith and trust in what God has done for them in the death and resurrection of Jesus Christ.

The Christian life begins with Baptism. It then has to develop and grow. The local Church plays an important role in helping to guard and develop this gift of grace given to us by God. It is only within the worshipping community that this can take place. You cannot be a Christian without being part of the life and worship of the local Church.

To receive the full benefit from a gift, much depends on the person who receives it, as well as the giver. The gift of "grace" in Baptism needs faith and worship to develop a living relationship with God.

THE SACRAMENT OF CONFIRMATION

This is the second Sacrament in the process of becoming a full member of the Church. It is completed with the Eucharist. In the early Church, adult baptism and confirmation usually took place at the same time. Normally, we receive Holy Communion after Confirmation.

Confirmation in the NT. Acts of the Apostles 8.14–17: "When the Apostles at Jerusalem heard that Samaria had received the Word of God, they sent to them Peter and John, who came down and prayed for them that they might receive the Holy Spirit; for it had not yet fallen on any of them, but they had only been baptised in the name of the Lord Jesus. Then they laid their hands on them and they received the Holy Spirit."

The meaning of Confirmation. Confirm means to make firm, strengthen or complete. Confirmation strengthens the grace already given in Baptism. A special mark or "character" is made on the soul which can never be removed.

In Baptism, we are united with Christ. We become children of God, and inheritors with Christ of the Kingdom of Heaven.

In Confirmation, the Spirit gives special skills to each of us. These gifts can be used (or not used) to share in the work of the Church:

Gifts of the Spirit. 1 Corinthians 12.4-11: "There are a variety of gifts, but the same Spirit; and there are varieties of service, but the same Lord; and there are varieties of working, but it is the same God who inspires them all in every one. To each is given the manifestation of the Spirit for the common good. To one is given through the Spirit the utterance of wisdom, and to another the utterance of knowledge according to the same Spirit, to another faith by the same spirit, to another gifts of healing by the one Spirit, to another the working of miracles, to another prophecy, to another the ability to distinguish between spirits, to another various kinds of tongues, to another the interpretation of tongues. All these are inspired by one and the same Spirit, who apportions to each one individually as He wills."

When a baby is baptised, Godparents make promises on his or her behalf. These same promises are made again at Confirmation by each candidate. Confirmation is an opportunity for each to make his or her own act of commitment to God.

The outward and visible sign of Confirmation. "The matter" of this Sacrament is the anointing oil. The Bishop extends his hands towards the candidates as he prays for the Holy Spirit to come upon them. The Bishop also lays his hands on the head of each candidate.

"The form" is the correct words spoken by the Bishop – "Confirm, O Lord, your servant … with the Holy Spirit". The Bishop makes the Sign of the Cross with oil on the candidates forehead, and he says "Mary/John, be sealed with the gift of the Holy Spirit".

The Bishop blesses the three oils on Maundy Thursday at a Chrism Mass. They are the Oil of Catecumenate for Baptism, the Oil of Chrism for Confirmation, and the Oil for the Anointing of the Sick.

The inward and spiritual grace at Confirmation. The Holy Spirit enriches the soul of the candidate with inner grace. This is a special spiritual strengthening, which helps us to remain faithful to Christ.

Preparation for Confirmation. Young people can be confirmed when they are old enough to understand some of the benefits which they will receive from the Sacrament. Instruction is given before Confirmation, usually about the nature and effect of the Sacraments. The Creed, the Lord's Prayer, and the Commandments are explained. The candidates are helped with the Spiritual Life and understanding the Eucharist.

The candidates are asked "Do you turn to Christ? Do you repent of your sins? Do you renounce evil?" Confirmation should be received when the candidate is in a state of grace – that is, when he or she is in a right relationship with God. Thus each candidate is encouraged to make a confession to a priest before receiving the Sacrament of Confirmation. This is done either in a General Confession (perhaps at the Rehearsal?) or an individual Confession.

The effects of Confirmation. It encourages us to do our share to help the work of the Church. It is in some ways like Ordination for a Priest. Confirmation makes us "soldiers and servants of Christ" for the rest of our lives on earth.

THE SACRAMENT OF THE EUCHARIST

Different names. Eucharist means Thanksgiving. Holy Communion is sharing of holy things. Mass (from the Latin word) means: "you are sent out". Other names include The Lord's Supper, The Breaking of the Bread, The Liturgy.

Jewish roots of the Eucharist. Jesus celebrated the first Eucharist in the Upper Room at Jerusalem on Holy ('Maundy') Thursday. That Last Supper with His Apostles was the Jewish Passover Festival, which is rich in Jewish history. It celebrated the escape of the Israelites from their slavery in Egypt. Christ is our Passover, who has been sacrificed for us. His blood was shed on the Cross so that we can escape from the slavery of sin and death.

Jesus gave a new significance to the Passover meal. A lamb was normally sacrificed at the Passover Festival. Jesus made a dramatic change. He took a piece of bread and said – "This is my body". Jesus put Himself in place of the lamb. He was anticipating His own death on the Cross on the next morning. When Supper was over, He took a cup of wine and said – "This is my Blood of the Covenant, which is poured out for many for the forgiveness of sins". (St Matthew 26.27). The Old Covenant between God and Israel was sealed by the blood of an animal sacrifice. This New Covenant was to be sealed by the Blood of Christ on the Cross.

"Do this in memory of me." The Church through the centuries has looked back to the words of Jesus at the Last Supper as the foundation of the Eucharist. The Church has obeyed this direct command of Jesus, given at a most significant time in his life. Soon after the Resurrection, obeying this command became the central act of worship of the Church. It has been celebrated in unbroken continuity from the time of Jesus.

Christians gather together at the Eucharist to receive the benefits which Christ won for us on the Cross. The priest takes the bread and the cup, just as Jesus did at the Last Supper. But it is not just a dramatic remembering or re-telling of what Jesus did long ago. The Passover was a memorial, not simply to "remember" the Jewish escape from slavery (The Exodus). The events of the past become a reality in the present time in the celebration of the Passover. In the same way, Christians are brought into the death and resurrection of Jesus in the Eucharist. This is not just a remembering and re-telling of what happened at Calvary. By the power of the Holy Spirit, we actually share in the death and resurrection of Jesus as a present reality.

The Sacrament of the Eucharist. For those who hold to the traditional teaching of the Church, the "Minister" of the Sacrament is an ordained male priest. The "Form" is the correct words as used by Jesus at the Last Supper. The "Matter" is the bread and wine.

The Sacrifice of the Mass. From earliest times, the Eucharist has been thought of as some kind of sacrifice. The Jews killed animals and offered them as sacrifices to put themselves right with God. In the Old Testament, Abraham believed that God wanted him to offer his only son Isaac as a sacrifice to God (Genesis 22.1-19). At the last moment, God provided a lamb for the sacrifice. Jesus Christ offered Himself as "the Lamb of God". He is the "one, perfect and sufficient sacrifice" freely offered for the sins of the whole world.

No blood is shed in the Eucharist. It is a bloodless spiritual sacrifice. Christ's one sacrifice at Calvary cannot be repeated. In the Eucharist, God's powerful acts in Christ are proclaimed and made a present reality. It is a "perpetual memorial of his precious death and passion". Through this memorial, Christians are united with the sacrifice of Christ. They are also united with other Christians around the world, and with Christians who loved and served God in former generations. The Eucharist means "Thanksgiving". It is our thanksgiving for Christ's self sacrifice and the benefits He won for us. In the Eucharist, the Church is united with the sacrifice of Christ, which He continually offers to His Father in Heaven. We need to be part of it. Christ's sacrifice is made a reality every time that the Eucharist is celebrated.

The Body and Blood of Christ. There is no point in celebrating the Eucharist unless a vital change does take place in the bread and wine. Christians have recognised the Risen Christ in the "breaking of the bread" through the centuries. We celebrate the real presence of the Lord in this Sacrament. Bread and wine are changed by the Holy Spirit, working through the priest and congregation. The Eucharist is Christ's greatest gift to the Church. In it, there is an "exchange of gifts". We offer ourselves to God, and He gives His life to us.

THE SACRAMENT OF MATRIMONY

Marriage for a Christian is much more than a legal contract between a man and a woman. In Christian marriage, the third party involved is God, both on the wedding day and throughout the marriage.

The Minister. The ordained priest is not "the Minister" who celebrates this Sacrament. The Minister is the couple themselves. The priest is there as a witness, and to give God's Blessing on the marriage.

The bride and groom make their vows to each other in the presence of God. The Lord is much more than an unseen witness. God gives a precious and special element to Christian Marriage. The priest quotes the words of Jesus – St Mark 10.9: "Those whom God hath joined together ..." Those words are the foundation of Christian marriage. There is truth in the old saying – "Marriages are made in Heaven."

Outward and Visible Sign of the Sacrament. The wedding ring is an outward and visible sign that the couple have been joined together by God. The ring reminds them of the gift of God's grace which they receive through the Sacrament. That grace – or inward spiritual strength – is unseen, but it is available to the couple throughout their married life. This grace can be constantly renewed. The grace of God helps them to fulfil their responsibilities to each other, and to deepen their love. Their human love is caught up in the love of God. 1 John 4.16: "God is love, and he who abides in love abides in God, and God abides in him."

A lifelong union. Christian marriage is a lifelong union of one man and one woman, according to the will of God. It is a bond sealed by God, which cannot be ended "till death us do part".

Marriage in the Bible. Great importance is given to the marriage relationship in the Scriptures. Here are some examples –

Genesis 1.27 God created man in His own image; male and female He created them. God blessed them and said "Be fruitful and multiply".

Exodus 20.14: "You shall not commit adultery."

Exodus 20.17: "You shall not covet your neighbour's wife."

The prophet Hosea compares the relationship between God and His chosen People in terms of a marriage relationship (Hosea 1.2-3; 3.1-5). Jesus gives great prominence to marriage (St Matthew 19.3-12). Ephesians 5.21-33: St Paul compares the union of husband and wife with the relationship between Christ and His Church. St Paul writes "Wives, be subject to your husbands, as to the Lord." This seems difficult with our modern view of equality. St Paul also puts the other side (v 25) "Husbands, love your wives, as Christ loved the Church and gave himself up for her." Christ in fact died for the Church. Jesus commanded His followers to love God and to love their neighbours. The love of husband and wife is to be a sign of the love between Christ and His Church.

The Marriage Contract. A man and a woman enter a marriage contract of their own free will. They are not forced to marry. They publicly and freely express their intention for it to happen. Then the bride and groom make an agreement to give themselves to each other, physically, emotionally, financially and in friendship, throughout their earthly lives. This agreement unites bride and groom in marriage. Freely given consent is vital. Without it, there is no valid marriage. This agreement is fulfilled as they become one flesh, and this needs to be constantly renewed.

Difficulties in Marriage. As time passes, the couple often discover faults in each other, which were not noticed or important before the marriage. The arrival of a baby can cause problems. The housework and many chores have to be done (by whom?). The couple have to work at their relationship. Time has to be made for each other, as well as for separate activities. Marriage is not about trying to bring about a change in a partner. It is a lifelong union, "for better for worse," and it includes forgiveness, toleration and respect for the other's point of view. Learning to communicate is important. Marriage is about trust and faithfulness and above all, about love.

Ephesians 4.26: "Do not let the sun go down on your anger."
1 Corinthians 13: It is helpful to read this chapter from time to time.

Why should people marry rather than live together? Security for husband, wife, and children, and a permanence of the relationship. It enables love to develop and grow. Above all, marriage is the will of God, particularly for Christians.

65

THE SACRAMENT OF ORDINATION

How did the ordained ministry begin? The Priesthood is not a human invention. It has its origins in Jesus Christ, our great High Priest. Before He ascended to Heaven, He appointed and commissioned the Twelve Apostles. He said to Simon: "You are Peter and on this rock I will build my Church, and the powers of death shall not prevail against it. I will give you the keys of the Kingdom of Heaven, and whatever you bind on earth shall be bound in Heaven, and whatever you lose on earth shall be loosed in Heaven" (St Matthew 16.18-19). Jesus commissioned Peter: "Feed my lambs. Feed my sheep" (St John 21.15-19). Jesus said: "You did not chose me, but I chose you and appointed you that you should go and bear fruit, and that your fruit should abide" (St John 15.16).

The Apostolic Succession. Before the Apostles died, God chose additional men to continue His work. The Apostles ordained their successors as bishops. They in their turn laid their hands on their successors.

The Threefold Ministry of Bishops, Priests and Deacons. This pattern developed very early in the life of the Church into more or less its present form. It is something which we have received, and has stood the test of time.

The ordination ("consecration") of a Bishop. From earliest times, three bishops (at least) have been involved in ordaining a new bishop. One is normally the Metropolitan (the Archbishop of the Province). Thus Our Lord's commission continues to the present day. The Apostolic Succession guarantees the validity of the ordained ministry. The authority of Christ guarantees that the Sacraments are valid channels of the grace of God.

What are the functions of a Bishop?
(1) The bishop is the guardian of the faith, first committed by Christ to the Apostles.
(2) He is a sign of the unity of the worldwide (catholic) Church.
(3) The Bishop has a "teaching office" (task) to proclaim the Gospel and to teach the faith to priests and lay people.
(4) The Bishop has a "pastoral office". He is a shepherd and pastor of the people of his diocese.

(5) The bishop has a "priestly office" and he can celebrate all seven Sacraments of the Church.

A bishop is ordained to take charge of a "diocese," or to assist the diocesan bishop.

Ordination of a Priest. The priest receives Holy Orders from God, through the laying on of hands with prayer by a duly consecrated bishop. The other priests attending the ordination also lay their hands on the head of the priest being ordained.

What are the main functions of the Priest?

(1) Christ commanded His Apostles at the Last Supper to celebrate the Eucharist. The priest shares in the ministry of the bishop. The function of the priest is most fully expressed in celebrating the Eucharist.

(2) Christ gave power and authority to the Apostles to forgive the sins of those who are penitent. Priests share in this ministry.

(3) The priest is given the power to Bless, and to administer the Sacraments of Baptism, Marriage, and the Anointing of the sick.

(4) He is to proclaim the Gospel, and expound the Word of God.

(5) He is called to "the ceaseless ministry of intercession". Prayer is a vital part of the life and ministry of every priest.

(6) He has to equip lay people for their ministry and witness.

Ordination of a Deacon. This is again done by a duly consecrated bishop, by the laying on of hands with prayer. It is usually the first step in becoming a priest (though some remain as a deacon throughout their ministry).

What are the functions of a Deacon? A deacon performs some priestly functions, but he cannot celebrate the Eucharist, pronounce the Absolution and the Blessing. Deacons are mentioned in the Acts of the Apostles (Acts 6.1-6).

The Sacrament of Ordination. An indelible character is given at ordination. The outward and visible sign ("the matter") is the laying on of hands with prayer by the bishop. The "form" is the use of the correct words in the service. Inward and spiritual grace and power are given to perform the sacred duties of the ordained ministry.

THE SACRAMENT OF ANOINTING

In His great love for us, God wants health and wholeness for all people. Exodus 15.26: "I am the Lord, your healer."

Jesus is the Healer. During His earthly ministry, Jesus spent much time healing the sick mainly by laying His hands on them. Many healing miracles are recorded in the Gospels. St John 10.10 – Jesus said "I came that they may have life, and have it abundantly."

Jesus gave power to the Apostles to heal. He sent out the Twelve. St Matthew 10.7-8: "Preach as you go, saying, The Kingdom of Heaven is at hand. Heal the sick …"
St Mark 6.7: Jesus sent them out "two by two, and gave them authority over the unclean spirits."
St Mark 6.13: "and they cast out many demons, and anointed with oil many that were sick and healed them."

St Mark 16.18: "They will lay their hands on the sick; and they will recover." (These words are not in some ancient versions of St Mark, but healing was undoubtedly important in the early Church).

After Jesus finished His earthly ministry, the Apostles continued his work of healing. But over the centuries, the anointing of the sick died out. It was limited to preparation for death (called Extreme Unction). During the twentieth century, the Church slowly started to use this Sacrament again for its original purpose.

The Sacrament of Anointing. This Sacrament is for the spiritual and bodily relief of all who are sick. It is based on two verses recorded in the Epistle of St James (who was the leader of the Church in Jerusalem).

St James 5.13-16: "Is any one among you suffering? Let him pray. Is any cheerful? Let him sing praise. Is any among you sick? Let him call the elders of the Church, and let them pray over him, anointing him with oil in the name of the Lord; and the prayer of faith will save the sick man, and the Lord will raise him up; and if he has committed sins, he will be forgiven. Therefore confess your sins to one another, and pray for one another, that you may be healed. The prayer of a righteous man has great power in its effects."

The Christian Church was undoubtedly a healing Church in its early years. Anointing the sick with oil and the laying on of hands with prayer were inherited from the Jews.

The oil used is normally olive oil. It is blessed by the bishop at a "Chrism Mass" each year, usually on Maundy Thursday.

Anointing and the Laying on of Hands is normally (but not always) done in the Eucharist – either in Church or at a home. The length of the service is much shorter at a home.

The outward and visible sign of the anointing (the Matter) is the sign of the Cross, made with the oil on the forehead (and sometimes on the back of the hands). Prayers are always used at an anointing, in the form of words (the Form) approved by the Church.

With anointing, there must be a desire for healing. There must be faith in the healing power of Jesus.

The effects of the Anointing. The inward and spiritual side of the Sacrament is the unseen healing grace given by the Holy Spirit. This brings healing and wholeness and inner strength to body and soul. Christ Himself is present, and Christ is the Healer in this Sacrament.

Sometimes the person is restored to health. Sometimes it is a healing of the soul, before the sick person goes on into God's nearer presence. Anointing brings the assurance of God's love and goodness. Saint Paul tells us that "nothing can separate us from the love of God in Christ Jesus".

Sin and evil and sickness. In the Gospels, healing and forgiveness are closely connected. Healing often comes as a result of forgiveness. St Mark 6.13: Jesus said "My son, your sins are forgiven" and he was healed.

A General Confession of Sins is usually included in the service – but the sick person can make a private confession if this is required.
The forgiveness of sins in this sacrament can give enormous relief of mind and soul for the sick person. This in itself can be a powerful factor in bringing health and wholeness.

THE SACRAMENT OF ABSOLUTION (PENANCE)

Sin separates us from God and His Church. We sin because of our weakness, and our decisions to chose what is against God's will. Sin is a deliberate rejection of God's Love and God's Laws. The more we grow in faith, the more we become aware of our sins, and our need for God's forgiveness. Jesus Christ offered Himself to His Heavenly Father as the perfect sacrifice for our sins. His offering of Himself on the Cross makes it possible for us to ask God to forgive our sins.

How do we receive God's forgiveness? It must be clearly stated that only God can forgive our sins. There are three ways in which we can ask God for forgiveness.

First, we can tell God about our sins in our private prayers, and ask for His forgiveness. We will receive His forgiveness in this way.

Jesus Christ gave power to His Church to forgive and absolve our sins. St John 20.22: Jesus breathed on them and said "Receive the Holy Spirit. If you forgive the sins of any, they are forgiven. If you retain the sins of any, they are retained." The Apostles passed on this power to forgive sins to the bishops, whom they ordained as their successors. The bishops pass it on to every priest in the Ordination Service, through the laying on of hands.

Second, we can confess our sins with the rest of the congregation in the General Confession at the beginning of the Eucharist. The priest pronounces the General Absolution – God's forgiveness for all who are present.

The third way to confess our sins and receive God's forgiveness is by making a confession before a priest. This is called the Sacrament of Penance (or Reconciliation) but is usually known as Confession.

Preparing to make a private confession. Careful preparation is required. It is helpful to look up in your Bible and read the following:

The Ten Commandments	–	Exodus 20.2-17
The Beatitudes	–	St Matthew 5.3-10
The Summary of the Law	–	St Mark 12.29-31
Our need for forgiveness	–	1 John 1.8-9

When you have a number of different sins on your conscience, it helps to make a list. This can be destroyed after the confession.

Questions to think about. It is good to think about your life: do I really love God? And my neighbour? Do I make time for my prayers each day? Do I worship God regularly on Sundays and Holy Days? Are there any other sins which I have committed? Complete honesty is required.

Repentance – sorrow for sin. We have to be truly sorry for all our sins, and to turn away from past sins. We need to turn afresh to God and to be reconciled with God, and with other people. This is not a single event, but a daily struggle against sin. It involves a change of heart.

1 John 2.1b-2: If anyone does sin, we have an advocate with the Father, Jesus Christ the righteous; and He is the expiation for our sins, and not for ours only, but also for the sins of the whole world.

An essential condition. In the Lord's Prayer, Jesus taught us to say: "Forgive us our trespasses (sins) as we forgive those who trespass against us." And: "If you forgive men their trespasses, your Heavenly Father also will forgive you. If you do not forgive men their trespasses, neither will your Father forgive your trespasses." (St Matthew 6.14).

The confession. You kneel down and make the Sign of the Cross. There is a set form of words which the priest will provide. The priest will give you advice ("counsel") and set a Penance – usually a prayer or Scripture reading. Then he gives the Absolution.

The "seal" of the confession. The priest will never tell anyone anything he has heard in the confession. If you committ a murder, he will probably try to persuade you to go to the police. But he will not speak of it himself to anyone.

The results of the forgiveness of our sins. John Bunyon wrote in Pilgrim's Progress that forgiveness of sins is like putting down a heavy load. Certainly there is usually a great sense of relief. There is joy at no longer being separated from God by sin.

SEASONS AND FESTIVALS OF THE CHURCH YEAR

This calendar of the Church Year is ecumenical, and is used by Anglicans and Roman Catholics. There are two parts of the Church Year. The first half starts on Advent Sunday, and follows events in the life of Jesus. The second half begins with Pentecost, when the Church works out and considers the consequences of what Jesus did for us.

Advent. The four weeks and Sundays before Christmas. It is a time of preparation for the coming of Christ, and it looks forward to His Second Coming at the end of time "to judge both the living and the dead". The traditional "themes" of Advent are Death, Judgement, Heaven and Hell.

Christmas Day. 25th December (the actual date is not known). The birthday of Christ. God is pure Spirit, and He took flesh when Jesus was born of the Virgin Mary at Bethlehem.

1st January. The "octave day" (8th day) of Christ's birth. Jesus was circumcised and given the name of Jesus. It is also an important Feast of the Virgin Mary.

The Epiphany of Christ. 6th January. This celebrates the showing or "manifestation" of Christ to the Gentiles with the coming of the Three Wise Men. Depending on the date of Easter, there can be up to six Sundays after the Epiphany, and before Lent.

Candlemas. 2nd February. Also called the Presentation of Christ in the Temple, and the Purification of the Blessed Virgin Mary.

Ash Wednesday. So called because ashes are imposed on the forehead in the form of a Cross (for those who desire it): "Remember you are dust, and to dust you shall return". It is the first day of Lent, and it is a day of repentance and sorrow for sin.

The Season of Lent. Jesus spent forty days in the desert preparing for His ministry. Lent is the forty days of preparation for Easter.

Palm Sunday. (The 6th Sunday in Lent). The beginning of Holy Week – the last week of the earthly life of Jesus. The Church celebrates His triumphal entry into Jerusalem and also His suffering.

Holy (Maundy) Thursday. (Thursday in Holy Week). Jesus instituted the Eucharist at the Last Supper in the Upper Room, and washed the feet of His disciples. Soon afterwards, he was betrayed and arrested in the Garden of Gethsemene.

Good Friday. A solemn day – on which we remember how Christ died for us on the Cross.

Holy Saturday. A day of sympathy, when the Church remembers the Body of Christ resting in the tomb. The Easter Vigil is celebrated in the evening when it is dark. (See Holy Saturday Vigil on page 47)

Easter Day. The Queen of Festivals. The Church celebrates the glorious resurrection of Christ from the dead. During the Great Forty Days of Easter, Christ appeared to his disciples to convince them that He was risen.

Ascension Day. The fortieth day after Easter. Christ bade farewell to His disciples, and He returned to His place "at the right hand of the Father" in Heaven.

Pentecost (Whit Sunday). Ten days after the Ascension. Christ sent the Holy Spirit to the Church. The Spirit came on the Apostles like "tongues of fire". Thus a Bishop's Mitre is shaped like a tongue of fire.

Trinity Sunday. The Sunday after Pentecost. The Church celebrates the mystery of – One God as Father, Son and Holy Spirit.

Corpus Christi. Thursday after Trinity Sunday. The Festival of the Body and Blood of Christ. It is not appropriate to celebrate this important feast on Holy Thursday because the Church is thinking about His betrayal and coming death.

Sundays in Ordinary Time. Also called Sundays of the Year – Sundays after Pentecost or Trinity. During this long period, the Church considers the consequences of Christ's "saving acts" for us.

All Saints Day – 1st November.   All Souls Day – 2nd November.

Christ the King. The final Sunday of the Church's Year.

TWELVE APOSTLES – PLUS TWO

St Andrew. A fisherman from Galilee. He was the first person to be called by Jesus. He brought his brother Simon Peter to Jesus. He was present at several occasions recorded in the Gospels. There is a tradition that he became Bishop of Constantinople, and was crucified at Patras on an "X" shaped cross. He is the Patron Saint of Scotland.

St Peter – Prince of the Apostles. A Galilean fisherman called Simon, who was the first to recognise Jesus as the Messiah. Jesus changed his name: "You are Peter, and on this rock I will build my Church". He was given the "Keys of the Kingdom of Heaven," and power to "bind and loose". After the resurrection, Jesus appeared to Peter alone (to forgive him for betraying Him?). Jesus then reaffirmed him as Leader – "Feed my sheep". He became Bishop of Rome, and wrote an Epistle and his "memoirs", which lie behind St Mark's Gospel. He died in 64AD in a persecution in Rome.

St James the Great. Brother of John, the "sons of Zebedee", a member of the inner circle and present at all important occasions. He was the first Apostle to die as a martyr, "killed by King Herod with the sword". Tradition says his body was taken to Compostella in Spain.

St John the Apostle. Brother of St James, he was one of the "inner circle". He leaned on Jesus' breast at the Last Supper, and on the Cross, Jesus committed his Mother to him. He was the first to understand the meaning of the empty tomb. He became Bishop of Ephesus, and Mary (mother of Jesus) came to live with him. Tradition has it that he wrote the Fourth Gospel. But scholars disagree about who wrote the three NT Epistles and Revelation of St John the Divine.

St Philip. Philip said: "We have found him of whom Moses in the Law and the Prophets wrote, Jesus of Nazareth". Nathaniel replied: "Can anything good come out of Nazareth?" At the Last Supper, Philip said "Lord, show us the Father and we shall be satisfied". Jesus said: "Do you not know that I am in the Father, and the Father in me?" Later he preached the Gospel in Phrygia.

St Bartholomew (also probably called Nathaniel). Jesus called him an "Israelite in whom there is no guile". Tradition says he preached the Gospel in Armenia, and died by being flayed alive.

St Thomas. Jesus said He was going to prepare a place for them "in my Father's house". Thomas did not know the way, so Jesus said: "I am the Way, the Truth and the Life. No one comes to the Father except by me." Thomas doubted the resurrection, and Jesus invited him to put his finger where the nails had been. He replied "My Lord and my God". Jesus said "Blessed are those who have not seen, yet believe". After the Resurrection, Thomas ministered in India.

St Matthew the Evangelist. A hated Tax collector who left profitable work to become an Apostle. Little is known about him. He is also called Levi. According to tradition, he wrote the First Gospel.

St James the Less. Scholars do not agree about how many are called "James" in the NT. He was "brother of the Lord", and leader of the infant Church in Jerusalem. At the Council of Jerusalem, he spoke in favour of allowing Gentiles to enter the Church. He wrote the Epistle bearing his name. He was stoned to death in 62AD by the Jews.

St Jude. (Not Judas Iscariot). A popular Saint and people ask for his prayers in time of trouble – "St Jude, pray for me." One saying of his is recorded in the NT – "Lord, how is it that you will manifest yourself to us, and not to the world?" Jesus said – "If a man loves me, he will keep my word, and my Father will love him, and we will come to him and make our home with him." He wrote the Epistle of Jude in the NT. He (and St Simon) died as martyrs in Iran (Persia).

Simon the Zealot. None of his words are found in the NT. He was a member of the Zealot party who wanted the hated Romans to be driven out by revolution. But force was not the way of Jesus.

Judas Iscariot. He betrayed Jesus to the Chief Priests for thirty pieces of silver. He realised his mistake, and then hanged himself.

St Matthias. He was "chosen by lot" to make up the number of the Twelve Apostles after the death of Judas Iscariot.

St Paul. As Saul of Tarsus, he tried to wipe out the infant Church. He was converted on the Damascus Road, and became the great Apostle to the Gentiles. He wrote many of the Letters in the NT. He died as a martyr in Rome in 64AD with St Peter.

PERSECUTION

The Three Wise Men did not tell King Herod where to find the new born King. Herod slew all children two years old and under. Joseph and Mary escaped with Jesus into Egypt. The whole adult life of Jesus was lived under threat of persecution, until He was finally killed on the Cross. Many have suffered since then for their faith in Christ.

St Luke 12.49: Jesus said – "I came to cast fire upon the earth." The coming of the Kingdom of God is a time for accepting or rejecting Christ. It is a time of judgement.

St John 15.18: Jesus said "If the world hates you, know that it has hated me before it hated you." Christians cannot say they have not been warned. Jesus knew that many of his disciples would face terrible persecution and death, because of their faith in Him.

Persecution by the Jews. Jewish leaders thought they had destroyed the new Christian movement by killing Jesus. When they realised this was not so, they stoned to death St Stephen, and St James was beheaded. St Peter was arrested. But this had unexpected results. The faith and courage of the Apostles served only to strengthen other Christians. Some fled for safety to remote areas, and others settled abroad. This was the beginning of the spreading of the Faith throughout the world.

Jesus predicted the destruction of the city of Jerusalem. That happened in 70AD, about forty years after the Resurrection. He also predicted the persecution of his disciples, and suffering for the Jews, and the destruction of the Temple. The final separation between Jews and Christians took place at this time.

Persecution by the Roman Empire. The Empire included all kinds of nations and peoples. Rome wanted something to combine all these races into one united Empire. They found the answer in the worship of the Roman Emperor – Caesar. The different nations enjoyed peace, justice and prosperity, and they were happy to worship Caesar with a pinch of incense. That was exactly what Christians could not do. The first Commandment stated – "You shall worship the Lord your God, and Him only shall you serve."

Christians regarded Christ as their King, and they refused to worship the Emperor. The government saw this as an act of disloyalty and thus Christians were persecuted.

Nero's Persecution 64AD. Rome was destroyed by a terrible fire. People thought the Emperor Nero wanted to clear away slum housing and rebuild the city. Nero blamed Christians for the fire. The atrocities which followed are recorded by the Roman historian Tacitus. Christians were painted with pitch and burned like torches to light up the Vatican Gardens. Some were dressed in skins and were hunted like wild animals. Others were crucified. Even after this terrible persecution, Christians continued in their faith and trust in Christ. The Church continued to grow.

The Domitian Persecution 95 – 96AD. St John the Divine was banished to the Isle of Patmos in this persecution.

Persecution by Marcus Aurelius in 177AD. Christians at Lyons and Vienna were punished because they would not denounce Christ. Some were tortured, and others killed by animals in the amphitheatre.

Persecution under Septimus Severus 201 – 211AD. These were very cruel persecutions in Egypt and Africa.

Persecution under Decius 249 – 251AD. Everyone was ordered to sacrifice to the state "gods". Christians refused and were persecuted until the Emperor Decius died in 251AD.

Persecution under Valerian 257 – 258AD. Christians were sent to forced labour and their homes were confiscated.

The Great Persecution 303 – 313AD. Under Diocletian, Church buildings were destroyed and Bibles burned. Many died in his plan to destroy the Church.

Other persecutions. Sadly we must note that Christians have also persecuted other Christians. Christians have persecuted the Jews.

Modern persecution. It is also a sad fact that Christians are still persecuted today, and often far in excess of former years.

THE MARTYRS

Persecution produced "The noble army of martyrs" who suffered death rather than give up their faith in Christ. These men and women, boys and girls, are a glorious witness to the truth of the Gospel. Many died in prisons. Torture was often used to persuade them to give up their faith. But the Church was not destroyed. The opposite was true – "The blood of the martyrs is the seed of the Church." The bravery of the martyrs won admiration from Christians, and from those outside the Church.

MARTYRS OF THE NT PERIOD. Stephen was the first Christian martyr. It is probable that all the Apostles died as martyrs with the exception of St John the Beloved Disciple. Many other Christians also died in this period.

MARTYRS OF THE ROMAN EMPIRE. A few examples:
Ignatius – Bishop of Antioch. (Legend – the child whom Christ put among his quarrelling disciples). In 115AD, in old age, he was thrown to the lions for his faith. He wrote seven letters (which still exist) on his final journey to Rome.
Polycarp – Bishop of Smyrna. He was arrested and urged to curse Christ. He replied – "I have served Him for 86 years and He has done me no wrong. How can I blaspheme my King and my Saviour?" He was burned alive in 155AD. (A letter about his death survives).
Justin Martyr. He was ordered to sacrifice to the "gods". Justin, with five men and a woman refused. They were beheaded at Rome in 165.
Irenaeus – Bishop of Lyons. He defended Christianity in his writings (which are of great importance today). He was killed in a vicious persecution about 200AD.
Agnes – A twelve year old girl, who refused marriage and consecrated her life to God. During a persecution in 304AD she was put to death by stabbing in the throat (a normal method of execution at the time).

MARTYRS OF THE MIDDLE AGES. A few examples:
Edmund – King of East Anglia. Captured by Danes, he refused to renounce his faith. He was shot with arrows, and then beheaded in 896. His remains are in Bury St Edmund's Cathedral.
Thomas à Becket – Archbishop of Canterbury. He defended the authority and ideals of the Church against King. Henry II. As a result, he was murdered by three knights in his Cathedral in 1170.

MARTYRS OF THE INQUISITION. The Inquisition was a Roman Catholic Court, set up in 1232 to persecute heretics. At first, the heretics were Jews and Muslims, but later included Protestants during the Reformation. Many were found guilty of false beliefs and were tortured, imprisoned or burned at the stake. It was abolished in 1820.

MARTYRS OF THE REFORMATION PERIOD

Protestant Martyrs in England. England became a Roman Catholic country again in the reign of Queen Mary 1553-58. 288 people were burned for not giving up their new Protestant beliefs. These included Archbishop Thomas Cranmer, four bishops, 21 priests, 51 men and women, and 4 children. Bishops Nicholas Ridley and Hugh Latimer were burned at Oxford in 1555. Latimer's last words – "We shall by God's grace light such a candle in England as I trust will never be put out."

Roman Catholic Martyrs in England and Wales. Between 1535 and 1680, many Roman Catholics were killed because of their faith in Christ. Forty of them were formally "canonised" (made Saints) by the Vatican in 1970.

The most famous are: Thomas More, Lord Chancellor of England. He opposed Henry VIII in his divorce, and was beheaded in 1535.

Edmund Campion, a priest, was hanged at Tyburn in 1581.

Margaret Clitherow, a butcher's wife, was accused of harbouring priests. She was crushed to death in 1586 at York.

St Bartholomew's Day Massacre. French Protestants (Calvinists) – called Huguenots – were killed in large numbers in many French cities between 23rd – 25th August 1572.

MODERN MARTYRS include:

Dietrich Bonhoeffer, a German Pastor murdered by Nazis in 1945.

Archbishop Oscar Romero, RC Archbishop of San Salvador, shot while saying Mass in 1980.

Martin Luther King, a Baptist Minister shot in 1969 in Memphis.

Ester John, a Presbyterian killed by her Muslim brother in 1980.

Wang Zhiming, a Christian Pastor killed in the Chinese Cultural Revolution in 1972.

Literally millions of Christians have been martyred over the centuries. But more Christians have died for their faith in the 19th and 20th centuries than in all the earlier centuries added together.

THE REFORMATION

The Church split in 1054. The Orthodox Churches developed in the East, and the Roman Catholic Church in the West. Further divisions were made in the Western Church by the Reformation (1517-1559). Problems which led to the break up of the Church had existed for a long time. Political leaders had their own motives, and very little of the Reformation was to do with reforming the Church.

Why did the Reformation happen? The Church sold "Indulgences" (forgiveness of sins). People bought them to shorten their time in Purgatory. Other things needed reforming. Priests were not allowed to marry, but (unofficially) many had wives and children. Most clergy were poor and worked as farmers in the week. Some bishops and Church leaders were very wealthy. They lived on incomes which could support many clergy. The monasteries were no longer centres of learning and devotion, and some were morally lax. Lay people were unhappy about the state of the Church and the worldliness, greed and immoral ways of many of the clergy.

Attempts at Reform. John Wyclif (1330-1384) and the Lollards wanted reform. They paved the way for the Reformation. The situation was not all bad. There were holy Bishops, Priests and Monks who wanted change. The Council of Constance (1414-1418) was called to reform the Church, but no major reforms were made by it.

Martin Luther (1483-1546). He was a German monk who protested in 1517 against the sale of 'Indulgences'. He believed that we are put right with God by "faith alone". He was excommunicated. War broke out between Protestants and Catholics in 1524. The German Princes were allowed to follow Luther's teaching in 1526. This was reversed in 1529, and Lutherans protested. Hence the word "Protestant". The Augsburg Confession (1530) created the Lutheran Church. Lutheranism spread from Germany to all parts of Europe.

Ulrich Zwingli (1484-1531). He was a Swiss Priest who was the Minister at Zurich. He persuaded the Town Council to accept Protestant teaching. Civil war broke out between Catholics and Protestants and Zwingli was killed in 1531. After his death, the teaching of Calvin was accepted. The Swiss mountain Cantons remained Catholic, but Cantons in the cities accepted Protestantism.

John Calvin (1509-1564). Protestants in France were called Huguenots. Calvin broke with the Catholic Church in 1533, and fled to Switzerland. Pastors trained by Calvin spread their new beliefs in France, West Germany, Holland and Scotland.

The Reformation in England. The break with Rome was at first political. Henry VIII wanted to divorce his Roman Catholic wife Catherine, because she could not produce a male heir. The Pope refused to annul the marriage. Henry then asked the Universities of Europe for their views. Archbishop Thomas Cranmer declared Henry's marriage to Catherine was not valid. Henry then married Anne Boleyn in 1533. The Pope excommunicated Henry. An Act of Parliament (1534) made Henry VIII and his successors the Supreme Head of the Church. Church taxes (£3,500 p.a.) paid to the Pope were stopped. Monasteries were closed (1536–1539) and their property and wealth went to the King. The Act of Six Articles (1539) upheld the Roman Catholic faith, but loyalty to the Pope became a criminal offence. Protestants were burned as heretics, and also Catholics who refused to recognise Henry as Head of the Church. Under Edward VI (the boy king), Protestant teachings were advanced. The first and second Book of Common Prayer were published in English (1549 and 1552). England became Roman Catholic again in Mary's reign (1533-1538). Many were burned as heretics in her reign. Queen Elizabeth I returned England to the Protestant faith. The Book of Common Prayer was published in 1559, and Catholics were persecuted. During the Civil War (1642-59), Bishops and Clergy were removed from office, and Charles I was executed (1649). The Church functioned again with the Restoration of Charles II. The Book of Common Prayer was revised and restored in 1662. Dissenters or Non-conformists wanted further reforms, and they became Puritans, Quakers, or Presbyterians.

Some results of the Reformation. It was good to have the Bible and Church services in English, and the Chalice at the Eucharist again given to lay people. Sadly, prayers for the dead were removed (restored by the Oxford Movement). The Apostolic Succession was not broken. New bishops were consecrated by bishops consecrated before the break with Rome. The "Counter Reformation" produced reforms in the Catholic Church. Divisions are sad and sinful. Through the changes of the Reformation, it is claimed the Church of England remained part of the one, Holy, Catholic and Apostolic Church.

OUTLINE HISTORY OF THE CHURCH

30 – (?) 100AD The Apostolic period.

30 – 64 Persecution of the Christian Church by the Jews.

51 Council of Jerusalem – Acts 15 – decides to admit Gentiles.

64 – 313 Persecution of the Christian Church by the Romans.

70 Jerusalem destroyed by the Romans.

260 Martyrdom of St Alban, the first known British martyr.

270 – 800 The Patristic Period (writings of the Church "Fathers").

285 St Anthony lived in Egyptian desert – the beginning of monasteries.

314 Council of Arles. Britain was represented by three Bishops.

325 Council of Nicaea – Jesus Christ is "of one substance with the Father." (Nicene Creed)

381 Council of Constantinople I – humanity of Jesus was confirmed.

395 The Roman Empire split between east and west.

401 The Roman Legions leave Britain.

410 The city of Rome was destroyed by the Goths.

431 Council of Ephesus – declared Jesus Christ is both God and Man.

451 Council of Chalcedon – Jesus Christ has two natures in one Person.

500 St Benedict founded a monastery at Subiacio (Benedictines).

553 Council of Constantinople II – condemned heresy.

570 – 632 Prophet Mohammed established the Muslim religion (Islam).

597 Pope Gregory sent St Augustine and 40 monks to convert England. St Columba died. He spread the Gospel in Scotland and Ireland. St Aidan started his mission in the north.

663 Council of Whitby.   The Church in England came under the authority of Rome, rather than the Celtic Church.

680 – 681 Council of Constantinople III: Christ had a human and Divine will.

732 Battle of Tours – Charles Martell halted the Muslim advance.

787 Council of Nicaea II – veneration of Images approved.

800 Pope Leo III crowned Charlemagne as the Holy Roman Emperor.

1054 The Great Schism between Rome and Constantinople.

1070 – 1160 The great cathedrals of Europe were built.

1095 – 1250 The Crusades to free the Holy Lands from Muslims.

1115 St Bernard established a monastery at Clairvaux (Cistercians).

1170 Martyrdom of St Thomas à Becket in Canterbury Cathedral.

1208 Francis of Assisi founded the Wandering Friars (Franciscans).

1231 The Inquisition set up to destroy heresy.

1305 – 1376 The Popes lived at Avignon, due to troubles at Rome.

1381 – 1417 Two Popes were elected, due to divisions in the Church.

1453 Constantinople was captured by the Turks (Muslims).

1517 Martin Luther starts the Protestant Reformation.
1532 Thomas Cranmer declared Henry VIII's marriage "null and void".
1534 Henry VIII declared himself Head of the Church in England.
1535 Thomas More & Bishop Fisher were executed.
1538 The Great Bible was published in English.
1539 The suppression of the monasteries in England.
1540 The Jesuit Order (Society of Jesus) was founded.
1545 – 1563 Council of Trent – Rome started the Counter Reformation.
1549 and 1552 First and Second Prayer Book of Edward VI in English.
1553 – 1558 England became Roman Catholic again during reign of Mary.
1559 Elizabeth I became Supreme Governor of the Church in England.
1633 Galileo was forced by the Church to give up his scientific views.
1646 Presbyterianism was established in England.
1649 Execution of Charles I – king and martyr.
1660 Restoration of the Monarchy and the Church.
1662 The Book of Common Prayer.
1673 Rebuilding of St Paul's Cathedral by Sir Christopher Wren.
1739 John Wesley founded the Methodist "Societies".
1789 The French Revolution. The Church was persecuted.
1829 The Roman Catholic Emancipation Act.
1833 Beginning of the Oxford Movement (Keble's Assize sermon).
1833 The Act for the Abolition of Slavery.
1845 John Henry Newman was converted to Roman Catholicism.
1859 Charles Darwin's "Origin of Species" was published.
1867 The first Lambeth Conference of Anglican Bishops.
1870 First Vatican Council. Pope's pronouncements are infallible.
1896 The Pope's "Encyclical" declared Anglican ordinations invalid.
1910 Edinburgh Conference – beginning of the Ecumenical Movement.
1914 Act passed to disestablish the Church of Wales.
1917 Russian Revolution declared religion was "opium of the people".
1928 Parliament rejected the "1928 Prayer Book" revisions.
1929 The Lateran Treaty created the free Vatican State in Rome.
1939 – 1945 World War II. Six million Jews killed by the Nazis.
1947 The creation of the state of Israel.
1948 The World Council of Churches was created.
1962 – 1965 The Second Vatican Council.
1963 "Honest to God" written by Bishop John Robinson.
1966 Archbishop Ramsey and Pope Paul VI "Common Declaration".
1969 The Synodical Government Measure created the General Synod.
1971 Anglican-Roman Catholic International Commission began.
1993 Women ordained as priests in the Church of England.
1998 Rome stated ordination of Anglican women was invalid.

LIBERALISM

There is a deep division in most Churches – Anglican, Roman Catholic and Protestant. Those who hold the original truths of the Christian faith are called orthodox or traditional. Traditional Anglicans accept the authority of Scripture and the Tradition of the Church, and the use of Reason. "What has been believed everywhere, always and by everyone" (St Vincent of Lerins 5th Century). Liberals reject much of the traditional Christian faith and moral teaching of the Church.

What is a liberal? Sweeping general statements are not always accurate, but they can contain much truth. A liberal is a person who believes in religious freedom. Each individual is free to pursue the truth as he or she sees it. This involves questioning traditional beliefs and moral teaching. They claim to make the Christian faith closer to the truth, and more acceptable to the modern world.

The rise of liberalism. The "Enlightenment" and The "Age of Reason" in 18th century encouraged people to question traditional Christian beliefs. Scholars in Germany and elsewhere challenged the authority of the Bible.

In the Church of England, a three "party system" developed: (a) Evangelicals stressed the authority of the Bible. Evangelicals divided into Conservative and Liberal Evangelicals. (b) Anglican Catholics re-discovered the importance of the Sacraments through the Oxford Movement (1833). Since the ordination of women (1993) Anglican Catholics have been divided. Orthodox Catholics hold the traditional Apostolic faith. Affirming Catholics "affirm" and accept liberal teaching about morals and faith, including the ordination of women. (c) Central or Broad Churchmen do not belong to any party. In former years, "High", "Low" and "Broad Church" were evenly balanced. In the 1970s, liberal teaching gained much influence and power in the Church. The Open Synod Group put forward liberal ideas in General Synod. The Modern Churchpeople's Union (founded 1898) exists to teach liberal ideas – and very successful it has been.

What do liberals believe? Liberals do not have a common set of beliefs – except the search of truth. Between liberal and orthodox, there is a wide range of beliefs. Liberals have freedom to make up their own minds.

Liberals seems to start their religious thinking from themselves and their own thoughts. Traditional Christians start from what has been "given" to us and what has been "revealed" by God.

Liberals reject "revelation" and "authority" in the Bible where they think it does not reflect the truth. They see much of the Bible as a fallible human record. The modern liberal Church is often in direct conflict with the Scriptures. Discerning the truth of Christ has led liberals to contradict the Gospels.

Some parts of the creed are rejected. But the Nicene Creed is used in the Eucharist – not as a statement of fact – but "as a kind of poetic expression of the faith." Changes in belief are made to present Jesus Christ in a more acceptable way in the modern world. Many liberals reject the Virgin Birth, the Resurrection and the Ascension of Christ.

Basic parts of the Eucharist are altered or left out. God may be addressed as Mother (not Father, as Christ taught us). Ordination of women; and the celebration of the Eucharist by a lay person (one not ordained as a priest). These are all acceptable in the liberal way of thought. Traditional views of a priest as a man "set apart" by ordination are rejected.

Liberals do not believe that God "took flesh" and became Man in Jesus Christ. Thus some liberals do not sing Christmas Carols! Jesus is seen as a good man, a religious pioneer and a great teacher. But the Cross and Resurrection are "foolishness and a stumbling block." Miracles and the supernatural are regarded with suspicion.

Liberals believe that people are naturally good. Human society will improve by its own efforts, and that progress is unstoppable. The traditional Christian view is that human nature is flawed. We need God's forgiveness and help to make progress.

Is liberalism a good – or a bad thing? It is good to think about the Faith and to use modern methods to study the Bible. Problems arise when clear statements in the Bible are rejected. It raises questions – How long will liberals and "orthodox" Christians remain together in the same Church? What is required as minimum belief for members of the Christian Church?

DOUBTS ABOUT THE ORDINATION OF WOMEN

Equal rights and opportunities. The Church of England made a decision to ordain women as priests in 1992. It is said that this is a matter of equal opportunities and natural justice. The Church promotes "liberty and reconciliation". The ordination of women was influenced by Women's Liberation. It is good for women to have equal rights and opportunities, but secular ideas and "political correctness" cannot dictate what we do in Church. God created us male and female. He planned different roles for us, and they are not interchangeable.

The "maleness" of God. It is said that the "maleness" of God and Jesus is not important. The emphasis should be on God becoming "human" rather than becoming "man". True, God is not male, but most of the picture language about Him is male. The language is important. We have no authority to change that picture language. Throughout the Bible, God is revealed to us as Father, and this is at the centre of our understanding. If the priest is to be at the centre of our worship, as the image of Christ, then it is important the priest is male. Christians understand the nature of God in terms of the relationship between Father and Son, in the power of the Holy Spirit. The Apostles were "Fathers" of the Churches, and we received the Sacraments from their successors in an unbroken male line for nearly 2000 years. God chose to become man in Jesus. Jesus is called "Son" of God many times in St John's Gospel. There is no doubt that Jesus was a man. We may not understand why God acted in this way, but this is what He did. Many doubt the wisdom of altering what is seen as God's plan by ordaining women as priests.

God is our "Father". This is not just an image, but a proper name expressing the nature of God in the Bible. God's final revelation is that His name is "Abba Father". He is our Father, and we are His sons and daughters. We enter into this relationship because of what His Son has done for us. Only a male priest can be an effective sign or symbol of God. Only a male priest can completely represent Christ at the Altar.

Changing the nature of the Church. It is claimed the whole Church made a major change to admit Gentiles (Acts 15). And if the Church could make a change then, it can do so now to admit women priests. But admission of non-Jews was not a major change. Jesus said: "Go, and make disciples of all nations, baptising them … " (St Matthew 28.19).

At that time, the issue was not about accepting Gentiles, but whether or not converts should be circumcised. Pentecost and the gift of tongues were about gathering in people of all nations. However, to ordain women is a break with the Church's tradition for 2000 years.

A period of discernment. The Early Church realised that Councils of the Church could make mistakes. Decisions have to be accepted by the people. Mistakes were made in deciding whether Jesus was God or Man, or both. It took hundreds of years to sort it out. A long period of time will probably be needed to settle the question of women priests.

Why did God wait so long before calling women priests? Had they been part of God's plan, He would have called them long ago.

A male priest is a representative of Christ. In every Eucharist, Christ is the celebrant. A priest is a visible representative and living sign of Christ. This sign is clearly seen in a male priest, but not so with a woman priest. A male priest can represent both men and women. They have done so through the centuries. No one doubts that Jesus is the supreme representative of humanity to the Father. If one human male can exercise that representative function, then each male priest can be a representative of all people, male and female. A male priest witnesses to the things about the nature of God, which are seen in the maleness of Jesus. A male priest faithfully represents Christ.

Some women claim – "We have a right to have our vocation tested". It is irresponsible to experiment with the Sacraments if there is any doubt. We have no "rights" with God. All need His mercy and grace.

No Authority to change. The Church of England claims to be part of the one holy catholic and apostolic Church. If that is so, it has no authority to change the ministry without the agreement of the rest of the Church, including the Roman Catholic and the Orthodox Churches. Anglicans only make up 5 per cent of the whole Church. To make such a change invalidates its claim to be "catholic".

Doubt and certainty. There is absolutely no doubt about the validity of male Priests. There will be continuing doubts about women priests until the end of time. Even the Archbishop of Canterbury, Dr George Carey has admitted: "I may be proved wrong." (28th October 1999).

THE ORDINATION OF WOMEN AND THE BIBLE

How far can the Bible help in the ongoing debate about women priests and bishops?

The text used to support the ordination of women is Galatians 3.28: "There is neither Jew nor Greek, there is neither slave nor free, there is neither male nor female; for you are all one in Christ Jesus." It is claimed that this supports women's ordination. It is true that both men and women are redeemed by Jesus Christ. Both are equal in the sight of God. But St Paul is writing about Baptism and salvation, and not Ordination. In no way does this support the ordination of women.

Statements about the authority of men over women in the Bible:
(1) "The rib which the Lord God had taken from the man He made into a woman." (Genesis 2.22).
(2) "I permit no woman to teach or to have authority over men; she is to keep silent. For Adam was formed first, then Eve." (1 Timothy 2.12-13).
(3) "The head of every man is Christ, the head of a woman is her husband, and the head of Christ is God." (1 Corinthians 11.3).
(4) "Wives, be subject to your husbands, as to the Lord. For the husband is the head of the wife as Christ is head of the Church, His Body, and is Himself its Saviour. As the Church is subject to Christ, so let wives also be subject in everything to their husbands. Husbands, love your wives, as Christ loved the Church and gave Himself up for her." (Ephesians 5.22-25).
(5) "Likewise, you wives, be submissive to your husbands." (1 Peter 3.1).
(6) "Women should keep silence in the Churches. They are not permitted to speak, but should be subordinate, as even the law says. If there is anything they desire to know, let them ask their husbands at home. For it is shameful for a woman to speak in Church. What! Did the Word of God originate with you; or are you the only ones it has reached? If anyone thinks he is a prophet or spiritual, he should acknowledge that what I am writing to you is a command of the Lord. If anyone does not recognise this, he is not recognised." (1 Corinthians 14.34-38).

Headship. These quotations are difficult, and may well cause offence. Social conditions have changed since they were written, and men and women are now equal under the law in all areas of life. Women often excel in what was once a man's world. Some achieve greatness in politics, business, the armed forces and elsewhere. Why not in the Church? Part of the answer is found in these quotations. What did they mean when they were written? What do they mean today? Whatever answer we give, we cannot ignore them, as they are in the Bible. Scholars disagree about their meaning and importance. The Bible was given to us by God, through the Church. Christian doctrine and the Creeds are firmly based on Scripture, and we cannot pick and chose which to accept or reject. The Church is still under the 'judgement' of Scripture. The Bible still has a vital place in the life of the Church. These quotations seem to indicate that women's calling should be channelled in other ways, rather than ordination. "Blessed are those who hear the word of God and keep it." We need to think more about the question – "What is the nature of priesthood?"

Women and Prayer. St Paul writes about women leading prayer: "Any woman who prays or prophesies with her head unveiled" (1 Corinthians 11.5). This is possibly about a small prayer meeting, but it does not support the case for women priests.

Women through the ages. Women have served the Church no less than men: Julian of Norwich, St Theresa and many women saints and martyrs. Unrest about the position of women in the Church seems to have come at the same time as unrest about their position outside of it.

Jesus chose only men to be Apostles. Do we really know why? Some claim He could not alter the traditions and conventions of the time. But Jesus did exactly that on many occasions. He made major changes in the Jewish religion, which He used as the foundation for the Christian Church. He could have chosen women as Apostles, including Mary. Priestesses were common in pagan cults at that time. Jesus always treated women as being equal to men. He chose a woman, Mary Magdalene (not Peter) to be the first person to meet Him after His resurrection. Jesus did not make a mistake by choosing men only to be His Apostles. Jesus spoke and acted with supreme authority. His birth and ministry were the greatest act of forward planning of all time. His decisions were right then. They are right now, and for all eternity. To doubt His words and actions raises doubts about their permanent authority and value for today.

THE THREE CREEDS

What is a Creed? The word "Creed" comes from the Latin word 'Credo' meaning "I believe". It is easy to recite the three Creeds. But they were produced by the Church only as a result of conflict and disagreements over a long period of time. From the beginning, the Church needed a clear statement of her beliefs. This is a short summery of how the three Creeds came into existence. There is only one Gospel of Jesus Christ, even though four men wrote it down. So too there is only one Creed, even though there are three versions.

In order to guard against heresy, the Apostles Creed had to be expanded into the larger Nicene Creed, and this was later expanded into the Athanasian Creed. Sadly, false teachings and heresy are still common today, even among members of the Church.

Early development of the Creed. Candidates were asked to declare their Christian Faith before being Baptised and admitted into the Church. The earliest statement of Christian belief is in Romans 10.9 – "Jesus is Lord". This was expanded to include a belief in God the Father, God the Son, and God the Holy Spirit. By the end of the first century, this statement of belief contained the basic teaching of the Christian faith.

The Apostles' Creed. This is the shortest of the three. The Apostles did not sit down and write it before they separated to spread the Gospel. The Creed was given this name because it contains a summary of the faith as taught by the Apostles.

The early forms were used by the Church towards the end of the first century. The final version as we know it today was only completed about 600AD.

This Creed is a summary of the great truths of the faith. It includes a belief in the Almighty Father, Creator of heaven and earth. Then it states the basic facts about the life, death and resurrection of Jesus Christ. It includes the Holy Spirit, the holy catholic Church, the Communion of Saints, the forgiveness of sins, and the resurrection of the dead, and the life of the world to come.

The Nicene Creed. The short Apostles' Creed was not enough to prevent the appearance of false beliefs (heresies). About 300AD, a priest in Egypt called Arius taught that Jesus was not God. Jesus was only an intermediary between God and the human race. The Son of God did not exist before God took flesh in the womb of Mary.

God seems to raise up leaders at the appropriate time to deal with problems. So a man called Athanasius – a Deacon from Alexandria – came forward to defend the traditional teaching of the Church. The newly converted Roman Emperor Constantine called the Bishops and leaders of the Church to a Council at Nicaea in 325AD to deal with this problem. Under the leadership of Athanasius, the Council rejected the teaching of Arius. They decided to enlarge the section in the Apostles' Creed about the Son of God. Jesus Christ is "begotten of His Father before all worlds, God of God, Light of Light, very God of very God, begotten, not made, being of one substance with the Father, by whom all things were made."

The Nicene Creed came into existence as a result of the dispute. It is still used in the Eucharist today – though it did not reach its final form until about 700AD.

The Athanasian Creed. Not written by Athanasius, but called after him to recognise the part he played in guarding the faith. The Athanasian Creed sets forth the truth that Jesus Christ was God, and that He was also fully human. It comes very close to defining the nature of the Holy Trinity.

This Creed is much longer than the two earlier creeds, and it is rarely used in worship. Even so, it is an essential statement of the faith.

The importance of the Creeds. The Creeds provide us with the vital truths of the traditional faith. They were formulated before the division of the Church into East and West in 1054AD, and thus they are accepted and shared by all branches of the Church.

THE TEN COMMANDMENTS

The Commandments come from the time when the Israelites settled in the Promised Land (1800BC?). They are still important today, but more is needed than Laws. Jesus transformed them by adding the two Great Commandments – "Love God" and "Love your neighbour".

1st Commandment – "I am the Lord your God. You shall have no other 'gods' before me". Satan tempted Jesus to worship him in the desert: Jesus said: "It is written, 'You shall worship the Lord your God and Him only shall you serve.' " (St Matthew 4.10). Modern "false gods" come in many different forms. It is a sin to put a "false god" between you and the living God. Christians are called upon to honour God not only in our worship, but also in our daily lives.

2nd Commandment – "You shall not make for yourself any idol. You shall not bow down to them or serve them". God alone is worthy of our worship, loyalty and love. Christians do not worship a crucifix, statue or picture of a Saint. We regard them with respect, because they remind us of what God has done for us. The sin of idolatry includes witchcraft, fortune telling, and astrology and attempts to contact the departed. God is a "jealous" God, who wants undivided loyalty. An idol is anything, which keeps us from worshipping God: e.g. washing the car on Sunday morning instead of worshipping God.

3rd Commandment – "You shall not take the name of the Lord your God in vain". "Jesus," "Christ," and "God" are not to be used as swear words. To use them in that way is blasphemy. "Let no evil talk come out of your mouths, but only such as is good for edifying, as fits the occasion, that it may impart grace to those who hear." (Ephesians 4.29) Our attitude towards God should be of reverence and "holy fear". You cannot love God and use His name as a swear word.

4th Commandment – "Remember to keep holy the Sabbath Day". God wants us to worship Him at least once every week. We keep Sunday holy by going to Church and receiving Holy Communion.

5th Commandment – "Honour your Father and Mother". It is easy to take loving parents for granted. Bringing up children is a major commitment, with sleepless nights and tender loving care, in good times and bad. A thousand and one things go into nurturing a family, and understanding those difficult teenage years. Backache when they are young, heartache as they mature. Children owe a great deal to parents, including love, honour and respect.

6th Commandment – "Thou shalt not kill". We only have one life, and it is a sacred gift from God. It is a crime deliberately to murder another person. Certainly, it is a very serious offence against the Law of God. This Commandment covers abortion, euthanasia, suicide, and the use of pain killing drugs deliberately to end life. Jesus said – "You shall love your neighbour as yourself." Also "Blessed are the peacemakers, for they shall be called sons of God".

7th Commandment – "You shall not commit adultery". This aims to uphold the sanctity of marriage. It is not a crime to have sexual relations with another person's husband or wife, but it is a sin against the Law of God. With so much sexual freedom in society, Christians have to guard against all forms of sexual temptation by thought, word and deed, and also by sight.

8th Commandment – "Thou shalt not steal". There may be a gap between the rich and the poor, and it is easy to see why people do steal. But it is a crime against the law, and a sin against the law of God. God wants us to respect all people and to respect their rights and property. He wants us to be honest in all we do. This includes not cheating, defrauding or stealing anything from neighbour or stranger, large company or small, hospital, school or anywhere else.

9th Commandment – "You shall not bear false witness". The need to tell the truth in a Law Court is obvious. Perjury can result in someone being wrongly punished, and punishment for the person making the false statement. The trial of Jesus before Pilate was a mockery of justice, and the Jewish leaders bore false witness against Him. Pilate asked Jesus – "What is truth?" In St John 14.6: Jesus said – "I am the Way, the Truth and the Life". God wants us to be honest with ourselves, with other people, and with God himself.

10th Commandment – "You shall not covet anything that belongs to your neighbour". To covet means wanting something which does not belong to you. Possessions do not give us joy. Happiness comes from love, and a right relationship with God and other people.

WHAT IS WORSHIP?

Worship is really an act of submission to God. It is the surrender of our will to His will. It is the offering of our loyalty and allegiance. In our worship we identify ourselves as belonging to God and His Kingdom. We acknowledge that He is Creator and Lord of the universe.

Worship is the offering of the very best that we are able to give. Worship means "worth-ship" – giving God His worth – giving Him what He deserves. It is offering to God what we owe to Him. It is the offering of our love to One who is Himself love.

Our offering to God. To worship is to love God. We show what God is worth to us by our regular worship Sunday by Sunday. We offer our adoration, praise and thanksgiving. Worship teaches us the faith, builds up the fellowship of the Church, and proclaims the Gospel. Above all else, it enables us to give glory to God.

Worship is a two way activity. We offer to God the best that we are able to offer. But we also expose ourselves to the influence of the Holy Spirit. God speaks to us through the Scriptures, the sermon and singing of hymns. The Holy Spirit challenges, encourages and inspires us. He reminds us what God has done for us. He pricks our consciences and helps us to confess our sins.

The Spirit feeds and unites us through the sharing of holy things. Our desire to worship is put into our hearts and minds by God Himself. He inspires us to worship Him in the first place.

The worship of our lives. Worship usually takes place in Church on Sunday. The way we live our lives in the week can also be regarded as worship. There is a connection between holy places and holy lives. We offer our daily lives to God in the Eucharist. Our worship helps to form the way we live our lives. Romans 12.1: "Present your bodies as a living sacrifice, holy and acceptable to God, which is your spiritual worship." Our behaviour and our daily prayers do affect the worship we offer in Church. God is Spirit. God is holy – set apart – and yet at the same time, He is very near to us.

Worship is not to entertain us. It is not even to stimulate holy thoughts and feelings. We are not spectators. Each has his or her part in offering prayers with (and for) the Priest – listening carefully to the Word of God – being open to the inspiration of the Spirit. Singing plays an important part, as we all make our offering to God with our voices. As we draw nearer to God, He reaches out to us in His Son. In our worship we respond to His love.

What is taking place spiritually? We open our hearts to the love of God. We expose our souls to the holiness of God. We consciously come into the presence of the Creator and sustainer of all life, in Heaven and on earth. We remember how God took flesh in Jesus Christ, and died on the Cross to save us from our sins. We become aware of the joy and power of the glorious resurrection. We are open to the influence of the Holy Spirit at work in the Church and the world.

How is Christ present in our worship? Christ is present through the Holy Spirit, when the Church gathers together to worship God. Christ is present in the Priest, through the Sacrament of Ordination. He is present in the congregation because of their union with Him and with each other in the Sacraments of Baptism and Confirmation. "When two or three are gathered together in my name, there am I in the midst of them." Christ is present through the Word of God in the Scriptures, prayers and sermon. Above all, the Body and Blood of Christ are present in the consecrated Bread and Wine of the Eucharist.

The greatest form of worship is the Eucharist. It has been the chief act of worship through the centuries. It is the only act of worship given to us by Christ Himself. We worship with angels and archangels, and all the company of Heaven. It is a foretaste of the Heavenly Banquet. The Priest offers the sacrifice of Christ to the Heavenly Father. The Priest is not repeating Christ's sacrifice. That was done by Christ once for all at Calvary. The Priest is re-presenting – or joining his offering with the offering of Christ to the Heavenly Father. This is shown when the Priest raises the Host (wafer) and Chalice (cup of wine) in the prayer of consecration.

Our worship expresses the mystery of Christ in our lives. It shows the real nature of the Church. It shows that the Church is both human and Divine. The greater part of the Church is unseen in Heaven, worshipping God, with the Blessed Virgin Mary, the Apostles, Prophets, Saints and Martyrs, and countless unknown Christians. Our worship here on earth is part of our preparation for sharing in the worship of Heaven in eternity.

WHY DO WE WORSHIP GOD SUNDAY BY SUNDAY?

There are a number of possible answers:

We worship God because within us there is a deep desire to worship.
We are made in the image of God, and this urge needs to be directed to
God. Sadly, the desire to worship is sometimes directed to an idol or
"false god" eg: pop-star, footballer, film-star, or motor car (idolatry).
We need to worship God in "spirit and truth".

We worship God to thank Him for creating us. God sustains us and
all living beings. By our worship we acknowledge our complete
dependence on Him for all things. We thank Him for what He has done
– and is still doing for us. We respond in "wonder, love and praise".

We worship God to thank Him for redeeming (saving) us. Our sins
separate us from God. The blood of Jesus was shed on the Cross to save
us from our sins. We receive the benefits which Jesus won for us on the
Cross chiefly through the Eucharist. Christ's sacrifice on the Cross has
broken down the barrier which separates us from Him. We worship Him
as our response to His redeeming love in Jesus. "O dearly, dearly has
He loved, and we must love Him too. And trust in His redeeming blood,
and try His works to do." Another hymn – "Love so amazing, so Divine,
demands my soul, my life, my all".

We worship God to strengthen the Church in its work and witness.
When we stay away, we weaken the Church, its worship and it's witness.
No one can take our place and make an offering to God instead of us.
No one can do the work for God which He wants each of us to do for
Him.

**We worship God to renew our faith and to deepen our love for Him
and for each other.** Our souls are hungry and we come together to be
fed with the Bread of Heaven. The spiritual hunger in our souls needs
to be fed.

We worship God to honour and praise our Heavenly Father. It is the
main way in which we can honour Him. We embark on a life-long
spiritual journey into the mystery of His love. Our worship is "for the
praise and glory of His name – for our good – and the good of all His
Church".

We worship God on Sunday to celebrate the Resurrection. The first Christians met on the "first day of the week for the breaking of the bread and the singing of hymns (ie the Eucharist). Faithful Christians have followed this example through the centuries. We can read the Bible and say our prayers at home, but we cannot celebrate the Eucharist and receive Holy Communion on our own without a priest.

We worship God to enter and share the spiritual experiences of other people. Our prayers are united with the prayers of the Catholic (universal) Church, and the Church through the ages. We listen to God's Word, and receive the Body and Blood of Christ. As we grow in faith, we are strengthened to share in Christ's work in the world. We become the Body of Christ. Our worship helps us to become "co-workers" with God to extend His Kingdom on earth. We worship to receive inspiration and forgiveness. We receive grace (spiritual strength) for the week ahead. We are challenged and prompted by the Holy Spirit. We seek God's will. We are caught up in His plan of salvation. We expose ourselves to the love of God, and we become channels for His love to flow through us to other people. Worship gives us a right relationship with God. Above all else, the purpose of worship is to give glory to God.

We worship God to acknowledge that He is our God. We worship Him regularly as He continues His saving work through our worship.

We worship God to come more fully into the presence of His transforming love. We grow in holiness (Sanctification). We are "changed from glory into glory, 'till in Heaven we take our place, 'till we cast our crowns before thee, lost in wonder, love and praise."

We worship God to show how much He is worth to us. Worship means "worthship". It shows where God is in our priorities. "Seek ye first the Kingdom of God." We become more God-centred instead of self-centred. We become more aware of God, and the needs of others. The main function of the Church is worship. All other activities are secondary.

We worship God to give meaning and purpose to our lives. It is the greatest thing we can do on earth. Belief in God without worship is worthless. Worship prepares us for life with God in Heaven.

VIEWS FROM THE PEWS ABOUT WORSHIP

The author invited members of his congregation to write about the question "Why do you worship God?"

I was born into a family that worshipped God. The 1662 Prayer Book Catechism states – "My duty towards God is to believe in Him, to worship Him, and to give Him thanks."
I have experienced so much joy, so many blessings and so much help in times of need, that I have never had reason to question the wisdom of trying to live according to that teaching, and as a member of the worshipping Church family.   (Irene Gulliver).

From childhood, I have always believed that a God exists, and that He is a good God, with whom one may communicate by "saying one's prayers" – a process started as a child.   When tragedy, illness or unpleasant events have struck (which they have) I have never been able to "blame God".   To be honest, I have never actually thanked Him for them, but I do thank Him, through His Son Jesus, for the good things in my life – love, health, good food and the created world, as well as money sufficient for our needs.   All these thoughts seem to be held together by "coming to Church", as is the belief that this is not the only life that we shall know.   (Tom Gray)

"Why do I worship (worth ship) God?"   I think this is what I am made for – to enter into a relationship with God, gradually to learn more of His greatness and goodness and to respond to it in every part of my life. "Why do I worship God in Church?"   Chiefly as a response to His invitation to meet Him in the Eucharist.   Also to learn more about Him in Bible readings and sermons, and hopefully to build up other Christians and to be built up by them.   (Anonymous)

Responding to your invitation to say why we worship God, I can only say very simply that for me, it is to join in prayer and praise, and to take part in the Liturgy of the Church.   I would, however, like more nobly to express my thoughts with the words of Jesus:
St John 4.24 : "God is spirit, and those who worship Him must worship in spirit and in truth."
And the words of King David in 1 Chronicles 16.29: "Ascribe to the Lord the glory due to His name; bring an offering, and come before Him. Worship the Lord in holy array."   (John Bailey)

I worship God because He gives me help in my daily prayers to live a cheerful and contented life, and also to give thanks for being so fortunate in having such a loving family around me. I enjoy talking to Him about any decisions I have to make. (Gladys Hatfield)

I worship God because I have faith in His goodness and mercy. He has guided me to overcome many problems. Who, but God, could think of such simple things to arouse and excite our senses – a beautiful sunset, glorious music, the touch of a friend, the smell of a rose, the taste of one's favourite food. I want to thank Him. (Anonymous)

There are three reasons why I worship God. (1) I was taken to Church regularly from an early age, and so habit and custom come into it. (2) Over many years, I have been lucky in being exposed to the preaching and teaching of many priests and the examples of friends and relations who have influenced me towards having a spiritual and worshipping side to my life. (3) We all have a desire or need deep within us to worship God. From earliest times, people have worshipped something – idols they made, nature, mother earth, the sun, moon, mythical gods – Greek, Nordic and so on. We Christians only worship our Creator and Redeemer, the one true God in three Persons, Father, Son and Holy Spirit. I feel deeply that I must do this. (Betty Webb).

I go to Church to worship God, and to give Him thanks for a lifetime of being guided and cared for. With God's help, large and small problems were solved with prayer. When I often thought all was lost, prayers were answered in unexpected ways. I have always tried to be loyal and do my duty to the best of my ability. There were difficulties, so I stayed near in prayer and sacraments. I still do, and hope someday to be re-united with family and friends, where Jesus reigns in glory.
(Connie Savage)

I nearly did not survive my birth. It seems that God has a purpose for my being here. I have always enjoyed Church, and feel I have found my true home at Emmanuel. Given all this, I can do no more that worship God and serve Him to the best of my ability, and thank Him for His mercies, and pray for His continued grace for the future.
(Florence Barton)

THE "SHAPE" OF THE EUCHARIST

The form of the service is based on very early records. There are three sections in the Eucharist: (1) The Preparation. (2) The Ministry of the Word. (3) The Ministry of the Sacrament.

(1)   THE PREPARATION

The Sign of the Cross. (See page 132)

The Collect for Purity. Sometimes said privately before the service. It is a prayer asking God to cleanse the thoughts of our hearts by the inspiration of the Holy Spirit.

The Penitential Rite. We confess our sins, and ask God for His forgiveness and mercy. The Priest pronounces the "Absolution" (God's forgiveness of our sins). Then we are ready to celebrate the Eucharist.

Gloria in Excelsis (Glory to God in the Highest). An ancient hymn of praise. It also shows our continual need of God's mercy.

(2)   THE MINISTRY OF THE WORD

God speaks to us through His "Word" just as He has spoken to Christians in former times. The Word "became flesh" in Jesus.

The Collect. A special prayer for the day, which gathers (collects) the themes from the Scripture readings

The Old Testament. The OT tells of God's preparation for the coming of Christ. We hear about the mighty acts of God in history and we benefit from hearing His Word in the Old Covenant.

The Responsorial Psalm. The Psalter is the greatest Prayer Book. Our daily thoughts and feelings are often reflected in the Psalms. We respond to God's Word in the Responsorial Psalms.

New Testament Reading. Usually from one of the NT Letters, the Acts of the Apostles or the Apocalypse (Book of Revelation).

The Gospel. We stand and face the Gospel, because it is the words of Christ Himself speaking to us through the words of the Gospel.

The Sermon – sometimes called the Homily or Address. It is used to explain the Scriptures and to proclaim the Gospel.

Nicene Creed. A statement and proclamation of our Christian beliefs.

Intercessions – our prayers for the needs of the Church and the world.

The Peace. A sign of peace is usually exchanged. It is an ancient custom from the time of the Apostles. We greet each other and show that our faith is genuine. (It may be exchanged later in the service).

(3)   THE MINISTRY OF THE SACRAMENT

Offertory Procession. Bread is offered to God, representing our work, and wine our leisure. God blesses them and gives them back to us as the Body and Blood of Christ. (The Offertory is not about money).

The Consecration Prayer. The priest re-enacts and re-tells the story of the Last Supper, using the words which Christ used. The bread and wine are consecrated by the power of the Holy Spirit. They are changed into the Body and Blood of Christ.

The Lord's Prayer. It challenges us to live a Christian life.

The Breaking of the Bread – (called the Fraction). Just as the body of Jesus was broken on the Cross, so the priest breaks the bread.

Agnus Dei (Latin). O Lamb of God, that takest away the sins of the world, have mercy upon us.

The Communion. The climax of the service – a meeting with Christ

Blessing and Dismissal. The priest blesses all present, and sends us out "to love and serve the Lord". We have been equipped by Word and Sacrament to go out and proclaim the Gospel by the way we live our daily lives.

PRAYING THE EUCHARIST

Our worship is the most important thing we can do in this life. Consider the awesome privilege of what is happening. The congregation are not spectators to be entertained. Ideally all present actively share in the offering of the Eucharist to God. Each person makes his or her own worthy offering, with silent and corporate prayers, praises, listening and singing. We also worship God with our bodies, by kneeling, genuflecting, and making the Sign of the Cross.

Preparation before the Service. Arrive early. Prepare to approach God in a prayerful way. Use the precious time before the service in careful preparation for worship. Then you may be able to receive the blessings from God which He wants to give to you. Encourage others to prepare properly by your example. Here are some suggestions -

1. Walk quietly in Church. Kneel silently in the pew. Pause for a while. Do not start praying immediately. The Psalmist said – "Be still and know that I am God." Relax your body and mind. Try to centre your attention on God. Be aware that you are in the presence of God.
2. Repeat a short prayer a few times, slowly. Eg: Lord Jesus Christ, Son of God, have mercy on me (us). – or – Lord, I am not worthy – or – Holy Spirit of God, come and fill me with your love.
    Think about what God is like – His mercy, goodness, forgiveness, His many blessings, His presence, His love. Look at a Crucifix/Cross.
4. Look back over the past week. Recall your failures and sins, in preparation for the Confession. Our sins separate us from God.
5. Pray for people kneeling near to you – their families – their work – those leading the worship – anyone talking and disturbing others – any visitors – your loved ones – relatives – friends – neighbours – yourself, your work and leisure. Bring all of these to God in prayer, and ask that the service will be a blessing to us all.
6. Have your own special 'intention' at every Eucharist. (ie, put into words your own special reason for offering this Eucharist to the Lord).
7. Read the passages of Scripture prayerfully and slowly. What does God want to say to you – and the Church – through these readings? Could you turn any of the Scripture into a prayer ?
8. Read the hymns chosen for the service.
9. Try to be aware of God's presence all through the service. A prayer – Heavenly Father, send your Holy Spirit to help us all in our worship. We ask this through Jesus Christ our Lord. Amen.

10. Avoid unnecessary chatter. "Before the Mass, speak to God. During the Mass, listen to God. After the Mass, speak to each other." "Silence is the gateway to the spiritual life."
11. Some use the Hail Mary, Angelus or Rosary before the service.

Confession. We remember corporate sins, as well as our personal sins – Is our Church friendly and caring? Do we all welcome strangers as we should? Make the sign of the Cross at the absolution.

The Readings from Scripture. Pray for the readers. Pray that the congregation may be open to hear the Word of God.

Sermon (or Homily). Pray for the preacher. Listen carefully. Think about the main points of the sermon later in the day or week.

Intercessions. Be aware of the presence of the Holy Spirit in the congregation, and with those for whom you are praying. Offer your own prayers with the prayers of Mary, the Saints, and the Church.

The Peace – a prayer for the peace of Christ to be with us all. Are you at peace with everyone present?

The Offertory. Bread and wine are offered to God. They represent our work, our leisure and time. Ask yourself – Am I making a worthy offering to God in each of these three areas? We bring our whole lives to God. Bread and wine are offered to God, and He gives them back to us as His Body and Blood. This is sometimes called 'the exchange of gifts.'

Personal Prayer. In any time of silence, be aware of the spiritual activity which is taking place. Before Communion – repeat the words to yourself – "Lord, I am not worthy to receive you. Only say the word and I shall be healed." Immediately after Communion, when you have returned to your place, offer your own thanks to God.

Send us out. We ask God to send us out to use our skills and gifts in His service. We take Christ with us. Our voices can speak His words. Our lives and actions can show His love in the world. He has no other body in the world but ours. Words above the door as you go out of a Church in Bristol correctly state "The service begins here".

WHY DO PEOPLE PRAY TO GOD?

There are a number of reasons why people pray to God. You may find one or more of the answers ring true with you.

People pray to God because daily prayer really does work. It affects the person who is praying, and also the person who is being prayed for. It can change situations. The results of prayer may not always be what we want or expect. But it is always effective. St Paul wrote – "all things work together for good to them that love God."

Christians are people who are searching for God. Regular prayer is a vital activity in getting to know and love God.

Prayer is not an attempt to persuade God to change His mind. It is not asking God to do something which is against His will. Rather, we pray to bring our wishes and our wills into line with God's will. Thus in the Lord's Prayer, we say – "Thy will be done on earth as it is in Heaven".

God created the universe and He keeps it all in existence. One day, God will "make all things new in Christ". In response to this belief about the past and the future, Christians believe it is important to pray to God every day.

God is unseen and hidden from our eyes. Prayer is a spiritual activity, which develops our relationship and friendship with God. This relationship is broken by our sins, but it grows stronger through prayer.

Christians believe that God is a God of love. Thus, if we develop a relationship with God through our prayers, we will be affected by the love of God. St Paul reminds us that "nothing, not even death itself, can separate us from the love of God in Christ Jesus".

Our souls are created to have a relationship with God. Saint Augustine said – "Our souls are restless until they find their rest in Thee". This deep spiritual hunger and longing in each of us needs to be satisfied. And the best way to meet this need is to persevere in prayer.

God wants us to pray to Him. Prayer is frequently mentioned in the Bible. Jesus Himself prayed to His Heavenly Father. He taught His disciples to pray. Jesus assumes that His disciples in succeeding ages will also pray to God.

The Christian life is built up by prayer. Just as oxygen is vital for the body, so is prayer for the soul. Christian formation takes place in us mainly through our friendship with God in prayer. Only in this way can the Christian life live and grow in us. To put this another way – In this way we become aware of Christ living in us as friend and guide.

Daily prayer is the foundation of the spiritual life. It is impossible to be a disciple of Jesus Christ without regular prayer. We need God's help. Through prayer, we are brought into the life of the only true God, Father, Son and Holy Spirit – the Blessed and eternal Trinity.

Through Baptism, we become children of God. Our prayers give us direct and personal access into the very presence of the Creator and Ruler of the universe. He is our loving Heavenly Father.

God shows His love for us in His Son Jesus Christ. He suffered terribly, and He died for us. In return, we respond and show our love for Him through our prayers and in other ways too.

Prayer brings its rewards. Prayer is not easy. Most people need to make a decision to persevere. But there are happy rewards for those who are faithful in daily prayer. Above all, we need to grow in our prayer life. We need to ask ourselves the question – are my prayers the best I can offer to God? The rewards include a growing assurance of the love of God. He is our loving Heavenly Father, and gives us inner peace. He refreshes our souls. When we ask God in penitence and in faith, He will forgive us all our sins.

Prayer strengthens our hope of eternal life. Death is not the end of everything. God gives us the hope of Heaven through Jesus Christ. And this blessed hope is built up through our prayers.

THOUGHTS ABOUT PRAYER

There are different ways of praying to God. Find a way which works for you. As the years go by, aim to deepen your spiritual life. Christian formation takes place mainly in three ways, through reading the Bible – Daily Prayer – and the Eucharist. All three are needed.

Starting to Pray. Remember that God is always with you. God is waiting for you to turn to Him. Become aware of God's presence. Speak to God – either aloud – or silently in your heart. Aim to create a friendship with God. Perhaps you could begin by saying the Lord's Prayer. Say this each day – at first only in the morning. Later on, you could also use it in the evening too. Tell God about the things which are on your mind. Ask yourself – What is God like? Think about this in your prayers. God is a Person. He creates us, forgives, guides, heals and loves us. Not even death can separate us from the love of God in Jesus Christ. Different types of prayer are based on the word PACTS –

Preparation. "Be still and know that I am God." Try to put yourself in the presence of God. You will know when it is time to begin praying.

Adoration. Think of what God is like – His goodness – His love – His mercy – His glory. Praise and adore God for His love.

Confession. As we praise God, so we become aware of our sins and of our need for His forgiveness.

Thanksgiving. We can thank God for His forgiveness – His love – and for so many other blessings.

Supplications. Praying for other people – those in Church – in your street – at work – home – relatives – friends – those in need – the sick – the dying, the departed. Only then do you pray for yourself.

How important is prayer to you? Where does prayer come in your list of priorities each day? Could you create a special time each morning and each evening for God? Your morning prayers may have to be short if you are going to work. But try to pray each morning, even if your time is short. Could you set your alarm five minutes early?

Difficulty in prayer. You may not always feel like praying. It can be a considerable effort. There will be times when success depends on discipline. Ask yourself – Am I serious in my desire to be a follower of Christ? In time, you will come to feel the need to pray regularly.

Same time – same place each day. The benefits of regular daily prayer cannot be over emphasised. It may be not always easy, but becomes more so with perseverance. We all suffer from tiredness, forgetfulness or lack of motivation. But prayer is our response to God's actions for us through Jesus Christ. The Lord's Prayer can always be used, even if nothing else. After failure, we can always say sorry, and start our friendship with God all over again.

Arrow Prayers. These are useful additions to our regular routine. Use them wherever you are. Eg "Praying the News" as you watch TV or read the paper. When you hear the bell of one of the emergency services – "Lord, have mercy on all those involved in this situation".

Prayer and the Holy Trinity. In the course of time, we come to realise that our prayers are not really our prayers. They are something which we allow the Holy Spirit to do in us. We open ourselves to the Holy Spirit. The Holy Spirit joins us to Christ, and He also joins our prayers and praises and thanksgiving with the offering of Christ to the Heavenly Father. We join our prayers with the ceaseless prayers of the whole Church, – with the saints and angels in Heaven, – and the Church Militant here on earth.

Prayer is an activity within the community of Father, Son and Holy Spirit. In His goodness, God invites us to share in this activity of prayer and fellowship through the Holy Spirit. Even though we do not understand it, we need to share in this activity of God.

Prayer may be a difficult area for us. We can think of it as praying with the Spirit, and allowing Him to pray in us and through us. Sometimes our prayers will be more about ourselves and our own efforts. In time, we come to realise it is more about the Holy Spirit praying in us. It is about changing from "my will" to "God's will". This is a slow process. We need to recognise when our prayers are selfish. In due course, our prayers become less self centred, and more God centred.

STAGES IN SPIRITUAL FORMATION

God calls us to share in His own life. He invites us to partake in the life of the Holy Trinity. He waits for us to respond to His love for us in Jesus Christ. Spiritual growth does not take place quickly or easily, because we are all liable to sin. There are stages in our response to God. The order and speed in which spiritual formation takes place varies from person to person.

Starting the journey. People come to God in different ways – perhaps by admiring some quality in a friend who is a Christian – or reading a book – attending a funeral – or by many other ways. God is like a sower who plants seeds of faith. The seed is a message or "Word" from God. He does not force us to obey. We may reject or neglect Him, but He cares for us. God wants all people to be reconciled to Him through the Blood of Jesus. God patiently waits for us to discover His love, and accept His invitation to follow Christ. The seed germinates in the dark, and then comes to the surface. The process involves thinking about God and getting to know something about Him. What is He like? How do I come into His presence? How do I approach God? Why did Jesus die on the Cross? What does God want of me? The action of the Holy Spirit on our soul brings us to God.

Some people come to faith before they are Baptised. Others are baptised as a baby and come to faith at Confirmation, or later. Faith involves trusting in God and then committing ourselves to Him.

Discovering Jesus Christ. This is an important step in the spiritual journey. People through the ages have been attracted to Jesus. He is the greatest teacher the world has known. We discover that the teaching of Jesus was mainly about the Kingdom of God.

Discovering the Church. The Church can be a problem for some people. They can discover Jesus, but sometimes they do not want to know about the Church. Christ created His Church to extend His Kingdom. God wants us to worship Him not as an isolated individual, but with other Christians, and with "angels and archangels and all the company of Heaven". The Church is vital in God's plan of salvation.

Discovering our need for God's forgiveness. As we grow in faith, so we become more aware of our sins, and our need of God's forgiveness.

We can pray for the repentance and forgiveness of other people. We need the prayers, support and encouragement of other members of the Church to help us on our journey. We share many blessings.

Discovering Silence. Learning how to be alone with God, and allowing the Spirit to work in you. "Silence is the gateway to the spiritual life."

Our spiritual journey or pilgrimage. The Church itself has not yet reached its destination. The Church is on a journey or pilgrimage to God. The story began with the call of Abraham, and it continues through the Christian era. Each Christian enters and shares in this spiritual journey. Each of us forms part of that great story of the people of God. What is your contribution to this "faith story"?

Discovering the cost of our salvation. Our salvation was won at the terrible cost of Christ's Blood shed on the Cross. What can I do for God in return for His love? Our first response is to worship – to offer to God a minimum of one hour per week on Sunday. We can increase this as we grow in faith. We must ask: "How much is God worth to us?" Worship is the best way in which we can thank God for His love for us.

Discovering Christian Stewardship. We come to realise that our time, skills and money do not belong to us. They are gifts from God. We are not owners but Managers or Stewards of all that God has entrusted to us for our lifetime. God wants us to use all His gifts in a responsible way, and make time for Him, family and neighbours.

Seven whole days – not one in seven. Another stage is to realise that we have to take our faith home, and live by faith during the week, at work, and leisure activities. Faith without "good works" is dead.

Changed from glory into glory. We are formed as Christians largely by the way in which we pray. Prayer can be difficult. The main thing is to continue faithful, even when God does not seem to be there. We can learn to ask Mary and the Saints to pray for us, and to join their prayers with ours. There is only a thin dividing wall between this world and the next. Sometimes we can feel that we are very close to the Saints.

THE LORD'S PRAYER

The disciples said to Jesus: "Lord, teach us how to pray". In reply, He gave them what is called the "Lord's Prayer" or the "Our Father". It contains different types of prayer. It is suitable for beginners and for those who have been praying for a long time. It can be used in the morning and evening. Like all prayer, it should be prayed slowly.

Our Father. It is God who creates us and gives us life. He loves us with an eternal love. God is always "our" Father. Never "my" Father. We become brothers and sisters of Christ, through Baptism. We are united in God's one family, the Church, through the Holy Spirit. Like vulnerable children, we are dependent on our Heavenly Father for all our needs. We can approach our Heavenly Father with confidence that He will always hear our prayers.

Who art in Heaven. God Our Father is also the Father of all the assembly in the glory of Heaven. We are children of eternity, and we can experience a glimpse of Heaven during our lives here on earth.

Hallowed be Thy name. The modern world has lost all sense of the holiness of God. So we pray that God's name will be kept holy and honoured and praised by Christians. We pray that all people will one day come to honour and glorify and bless God's holy name.

Thy Kingdom come. We pray that God's Kingdom will be established in the world, in our own hearts, and in the Church. God's Kingdom is about justice, truth and love. There is spiritual warfare in all of us. Either God – or evil – will reign in our hearts. St Luke 17.21: "The Kingdom of God is in the midst of you."

Thy will be done on earth, as it is in Heaven. We do not always wish to obey God's will for us. There are times when we prefer to do what pleases us. This is a prayer that we may understand God's will, and have the desire and strength to do it on earth, just as the angels and saints do His will in Heaven. It is a prayer for God's grace to help us. When facing the Cross, Jesus said "Not my will, but thine be done". St John 4.34: He also said, "My food is to do the will of Him who sent me, and to accomplish His work".

Give us this day our daily bread. We pray that God will provide our daily food and our other needs. We remember those who produce our food, and the tragedy of those without the basic necessities of life. Our spiritual food includes the Word of God in the Scriptures, and the Bread of Life in the Eucharist. For some, "Daily Bread" refers to a Daily Eucharist.

Forgive us our trespasses, as we forgive those who trespass against us. We are all guilty of sin, and each day we need God's forgiveness, and His grace to repent. It is not always easy to ask for forgiveness. Only on condition that we forgive others can we receive forgiveness from God. This includes forgiving those who have hurt or cheated or wronged us in any way. It means that we must not hold a grudge. St Matthew 6.15: "If you do not forgive men their trespasses, neither will your Father forgive your trespasses."

Lead us not into temptation, but deliver us from evil. God allows us to be tempted, in order to test the reality of our Faith. Temptation comes in many forms and disguises. Temptation is a time of trial or testing. Ask yourself: Is my faith strong enough to resist this temptation – however attractive or seductive the temptation may be? Do I knowingly allow myself to be in a place of temptation? Do I use all spiritual resources available to resist evil? Thus we pray that we – and all Christians – may be given "grace" to resist temptation, and be delivered from future evil. Temptation itself is not a sin. It only becomes a sin when we are weak or careless, and give in to it.

For Thine is the Kingdom, the power and the glory, for ever and ever. This "Doxology" was added later by the Church. The Kingdom belongs to God. We cannot enter the Kingdom by our own efforts, but only through His forgiveness, mercy and love. His power and glory are not visible to the naked eye – but one day, through His mercy, we will see Him in the glory of all His assembly in Heaven.

Amen. This word means – "May it be so". The cost of what we are asking is considerable.

A RULE OF LIFE

All who are Baptised and Confirmed are encouraged to remain in communion with Christ and His Church.

Christians are asked to play their full part in the life and witness of the Church.

Prayer is about developing a relationship and friendship with God. To make time to pray and to worship, you will need to work out where God comes in your list of priorities.

Many people find it helpful to make and write down a Rule of Life for themselves. The following thoughts may guide you as you work out what is appropriate for you.

Pray for the help of the Holy Spirit in making the Rule.

Important parts of a Rule of Life:

To worship God in Church and to receive Holy Communion every Sunday. (Go to a weekday service if you cannot get there on Sunday)

To receive Communion on major Saints Days and other "Holy Days of Obligation".

To set aside time for prayer every day. Offer each day to God in prayer.

To read the Bible regularly, and in a systematic way.

To give money in a regular and responsible way for God's work through the Church.

Other things to consider for your Rule:

To give some of your time and skills to help the work of the Church.

To fast for one hour before receiving Holy Communion.

To pray regularly for your bishop, your parish priest and for all who are connected with your Church.

To observe special days – Candlemas, The Epiphany, Ash Wednesday, Good Friday, Ascension, Corpus Christi, Assumption of BVM.

Before the service begins, make careful preparation to receive the Body and Blood of Christ in the Eucharist.

To attend additional services and events during the Season of Lent, such as Stations of the Cross, Lent Talks, and a Quiet Day.

To review your Rule of Life once a year during Lent.

To make a Pilgrimage to Walsingham, Glastonbury or other place of pilgrimage in your area.

To observe a form of self-denial on Fridays.

To make a formal Confession to a Priest. Many find this very helpful.

Need for self-discipline. Discipline is not always popular, but necessary. If we worship or pray or read the Bible only when we feel in the mood, then not much spiritual activity will take place. Jesus did not feel like going to the Cross, but He went through with it. "Lord, not my will, but Thine, be done." If we persevere in the spiritual life, it will lead to joy and inner peace.

Do not be too ambitious with your Rule of Life. It is better to start with something you can do, rather than aim too high and fail to keep it. You can always add to it later on.

The different types of prayer. Which are the most important parts of prayer – learning to wait on God in silence, Adoration and Praise, Confession of sins, Thanksgiving, praying for other people, praying for yourself? Try to develop your relationship with God.

Difficulties in Prayer. In one way, praying is easy – simply talking to God. Much more is possible. Do not be surprised if you have difficulty in praying. You may be tempted to give up. Try to persevere. If you do give up for a time, tell God you are sorry, and ask Him to help you to start again. Ask the Holy Spirit to help you in your prayers.

LENT

What is Lent? Lent is a Penitential Season of the forty days before Easter. Christ died to redeem the world from sin. Because of His death and resurrection, our sins can be forgiven, and our lives can be renewed. Lent provides an opportunity each year to prepare for Easter, and to reflect on its meaning. It is a time to think about the mercy of God and the love of God. Lent offers us many themes to consider.

Lent begins on Ash Wednesday. Christians should make every effort to go to the Eucharist on this day. Before Lent begins, Palm Crosses used in the past year are brought back to Church and burned. On Ash Wednesday, the priest invites those who so wish to come to the altar rail to receive the Imposition of Ashes. He makes a small cross on the forehead of each person, saying "Remember that you are dust, and to dust you shall return. Turn away from sin and be faithful to Christ."

Lent ends in the afternoon of Holy (Maundy) Thursday – before the Evening Eucharist of the Lord's Supper.

Lent is a Season of Penance. There is a big difference between the way of the world, and the way of the Christian. We need to be aware of the reality of sin in the world, and how far the world is affecting our attempts to follow Christ. Are we aware of the reality of sin in our own hearts? The light of God's love shows up all that is hidden in our hearts. It is easy to forget, or to pretend that we are all right in the sight of God. If we take our religion seriously, we must also do something about our sins, which separate us from God. Lent is the traditional time when we do this. (See The Sacrament of Absolution and Penance – pages 70-71)

Fasting in Lent? The Church encourages self-discipline in Lent. We need to exercise self-denial and restraint in many areas all through life. It is easy to deceive ourselves regarding the need for self-discipline. In a number of places the Bible encourages us to fast. Jews, Christians and Muslims all practice fasting as a good spiritual practice. Fasting is a way of purifying the spirit, and also of sacrificing something to the Lord. The purpose of fasting is not to cause distress, but to help us to resist temptation, and to strengthen the spiritual life.

The two main fast days are Ash Wednesday and Good Friday. For those who fast, one main meal, with two other light meals is suggested.

"Giving things" up in Lent. There is merit in giving up luxuries in Lent, such as chocolates, alcohol, tobacco. This reflects the spirit of penitence in Lent. The money saved is given to a good cause, and most Churches have a special Lenten Collection.

The Church gives up certain things in Lent. The Gloria and Alleluia are not used. There are no flowers and no organ voluntaries. Crucifixes, crosses, statutes are veiled with purple (sometimes in red from Passion Sunday). The contrast with the joy of Easter is great.

A change of heart. We say with our lips "I turn to Christ", but we so easily turn back to the world. We need a basic change of heart to alter the way in which we think and act, and to keep firm our resolve to sin no more. How do we amend our lives and forsake sin? Resolve to sin no more. Ask God for the gift of perseverance. Changing our heart and our way of thinking is not easy. It can be a long process, or a short one. We do not change and grow on our own, as all Christians are sharing in this same process. Change takes place as our souls are exposed to the Word of God, which consoles and challenges us.

Baptism and the Annual Renewal of Baptismal Vows. At first, candidates were prepared during Lent for Baptism at Easter. In addition, those who committed a 'grave or public sin' were excommunicated and separated from the Church. They were only readmitted and allowed to receive the sacraments at Easter after a period of repentance and penance. Today, Lent is a time when we examine our own consciences, and think about our commitment to Christ. Baptism is a very important Sacrament, and all the other Sacraments depend on it. Thus we think about the meaning of Baptism, and look forward to renewing our Baptismal Promises usually at the Vigil Service on Easter Eve (and also on Easter Day).

Planning how to use the Season of Lent. The Church usually has extra services: Stations of the Cross (See pages 118-119), Compline, and talks and discussions. Try to go to them. Use Lent to examine your own spiritual life. Re-examine your Rule of Life (See pages 112-113). If you do not have a Rule, Lent is a good time to make one. Find time to think and pray about how to use Lent (the time between Ash Wednesday and the First Sunday of Lent is a good time to do this). Observing Lent properly can help you to experience the joy of Easter.

THE PROBLEM OF INNOCENT SUFFERING

There is much misery in the world. Many are born mentally or physically handicapped. Countless people develop painful and incurable illnesses, dying in agony and despair. We also see the tragic results of natural disasters on television week after week. The sight of this undeserved suffering can be an obstacle to belief in God.

Christians believe that God is all-powerful and the source of all goodness. Others are prompted to ask: How can God allow suffering, as He is the source of all power and goodness? These are reasonable questions, and difficult to answer! Some people use the problem of suffering to argue against the existence of God.

Suffering and evil. Early in the Old Testament, people believed that suffering was the result of sin. Genesis describes how evil entered the world through the Adam and Eve story. They disobeyed God and ate the forbidden apple. Thus they were thrown out of the Garden of Eden.

Not everyone is satisfied with that explanation. Suffering and evil are not always the result of sin. Sin can cause suffering. Wars are the result of aggression, greed and hatred. On the other hand, think of earthquakes, floods, storms, and meteorites from space. Has God made a world with faults? Does God no longer love what He has created? Some believe that all creation was affected by man's disobedience of God. We have no real answer to these questions. They are mysteries which are hidden in the heart of God. But there are some attempts to provide an explanation. Job is one of the earliest.

The Book of Job. This has been called the "greatest work of genius" in the Old Testament. Job did not suffer because he sinned. He is himself an innocent victim, and he makes a direct appeal to God. Job's three 'Comforters' suggest that he is suffering because of his sins – or the sins of his family. Job knows he is innocent, even in the midst of his sufferings. Then God asks some questions which Job cannot answer. Job finally gives up, and entrusts himself to the mercy of God.
"I have uttered what I did not understand. I despise myself and repent in dust and ashes." (Job 42.36). God rebukes his three "Comforters" and He restores his health and riches. But no answer is given to the problem of undeserved suffering. Yet Job does reach forward to a deeper faith and hope, which will be more fully revealed in the future.

116

The "Suffering Servant" in the Book of Isaiah. Isaiah had a vision about God's plan of salvation through a Suffering Servant. His suffering was not the result of his own sins. He was blameless. He was suffering to bear the punishment due to other people. After the death of the Servant, God would reward and glorify Him. Many would come to know God through His suffering. These are deep mysteries, which foretell the suffering of Jesus on the Cross.

Suffering and the Apostle St Paul. St Paul develops Isaiah's theme of the 'Suffering Servant' when he describes the nature of the Church. We all form the one Body of Christ. Different limbs and members all contribute to the unity of the whole Body. United in that one Body of Christ, through our Baptism, we seem to share in Christ's suffering. Sometimes, suffering can bring out something good in people, and in the life of the Church.

St Paul suffered much in the course of his ministry. "Three times I have been beaten with rods; once I was stoned. Three times I have been shipwrecked; a night and a day I have been adrift at sea; on frequent journeys, in danger from rivers, danger from robbers, danger from my own people, danger from Gentiles, danger in the city, danger in the wilderness … (2 Corinthians 11.23).

St Paul suffered from an illness, and God did not answer his prayers for healing. "Three times I besought the Lord about this (illness) that it should leave me, but He said to me, 'My grace is sufficient for you, for my power is made perfect in weakness.' " (2 Corinthians 12.8).

Suffering and the Cross. Suffering does seem to have been part of God's plan. God took flesh in Jesus, and He fully entered into our human suffering. Jesus was an innocent victim on the Cross. This shows God's compassion for all who suffer innocently. All human suffering is bound up with the Passion of Jesus. Those who suffer actually seem to share in the suffering of Christ.

St Paul spoke of the Cross as foolishness and a stumbling block. But the Cross is also the power and wisdom of God. The Cross is a mystery and we have to admit we do not know all the answers. The Cross tells of God's love. When all has been said, all we can do is to trust in the goodness of God, and in the resurrection of His Son Jesus Christ.

117

THE STATIONS OF THE CROSS

Pilgrims in Jerusalem follow in the footsteps of Jesus along the Via Dolorosa. This is His last journey on the morning of His death. It began at the Praetorium (Palace of the Roman Governor – Pontius Pilate). It ended at the tomb of Joseph of Arimathaea. at Calvary. "Stations of the Cross" is a service in Church in Lent. There are 15 carvings or paintings on the Church walls showing scenes of Christ's last journey. A very short act of worship is held at each station. A hymn is sung whilst moving to the next station.

The readings and meditations help us to think deeply about the sufferings of Christ, and relate them to our own lives. It is a good Lent discipline to attend Stations during this penitential season. Here are some of the readings which might be used at each station.

Station One – Jesus is condemned to death. St Matthew 27.26: "When Pilate saw he was gaining nothing, but that a riot was beginning, he took water and washed his hands before the crowd, saying, "I am innocent of this man's blood; see to it yourselves". The people answered, "His blood be on us and on our children". He released Barabbas, and having scourged Jesus, delivered Him to be crucified."

Station Two – Jesus receives His Cross. St John 19.17: "So they took Jesus, and He went out bearing His Cross, to the place called the place of the skull, which is called in Hebrew "Golgotha."

Station Three – Jesus falls for the first time. St John 12.23-24: "The hour has come for the Son of Man to be glorified. Truly, truly I say to you, unless a grain of wheat falls into the earth and dies, it remains alone; but if it dies, it bears much fruit."

Station Four – Jesus meets His Mother. Lamentations 1.12-13: "Is it nothing to you, all you who pass by? Look and see if there is any sorrow like my sorrow which was brought upon me?

Station Five – Simon of Cyrene helps Jesus carry the Cross. St Luke 23.26: They seized one Simon of Cyrene, who was coming in from the country and laid on him the Cross, to carry it behind Jesus.

Station Six – The face of Jesus is wiped by Veronica. St Matthew 25.40: "Truly, I say to you, as you did it to one of the least of these my brethren, you did it to me."

Station Seven – Jesus falls for the second time. Psalm 69.3: "I am weary with my crying; my throat is parched. My eyes grow dim with waiting for my God."

Station Eight – Jesus speaks to the women of Jerusalem. St Matthew 23.37: "O Jerusalem, Jerusalem, killing the prophets and stoning those who are sent to you! How often would I have gathered your children together as a hen gatheres her brood under her wings, and you would not."

Station Nine – Jesus falls for the third time. 2 Corinthians 12.9: "My grace is sufficient for you, for my power is made perfect in weakness."

Station Ten – Jesus is stripped. St John 19.23-24: They took His garments and made four parts, one for each soldier. But His tunic was without seam, woven from top to bottom; so they said "Let us not tear it, but cast lots for it to see whose it shall be".

Station Eleven – Jesus is nailed to the Cross. St Luke 23.33-34: When they came to the place called the Skull, they crucified Him. Jesus said, "Father, forgive them; for they know not what they do".

Station Twelve – Jesus dies. St Luke 23.46: Jesus, crying with a loud voice, said "Father, into Thy hands I commit my Spirit".

Station Thirteen – Jesus is taken down from the Cross. St John 19. 34-38: One of the soldiers pierced His side with a spear, and there came out blood and water. Joseph of Arimathaea asked Pilate that he might take away the body of Jesus, and Pilate gave him leave.

Station Fourteen – Jesus is laid in the tomb. St John 19.38-42: They took the body of Jesus, and bound it in linen cloths with spices. Now there was a garden, and in the garden a new tomb, where no one had ever been laid. So they laid Jesus there.

Station Fifteen – Jesus is risen. Psalm 150.1: Praise the Lord. Praise God in His sanctuary. Praise Him in His mighty firmament.

THE SEVEN DEADLY SINS

Sin is an "offence" against God. Our Lord gave us two commands: "Love God" and "Love your neighbour". We can either follow or reject God's Laws. Sin involves a deliberate choice, and a free and willing rejection of His love and His law. Some sins are more serious than others. "Venial sins" are not a complete turning away from God. "Mortal sins" are more serious and deadly. The Seven Deadly Sins are not found as a list in the Bible. They were probably put together by St Gregory the Great (540-604AD). Having them in a group helps us to be aware of the different types of sin. It comes in many forms and disguises. It clouds our conscience and blurs the distinction between good and evil. We need to be constantly on our guard. We all know the difference between right and wrong. We are all responsible for our own actions. Christ won the victory over sin by His death and resurrection. Christians still have to fight "the world, the flesh and the Devil" through the power of His Holy Cross.

The Sin of Pride. Pride is "self love", and a love of one's own possessions and achievements. It is unhealthy to have an inflated view of ourselves and our qualities. Pride is the opposite of Christian love, which is directed to God and our neighbours. In reality, all that we are, and all that we have, ultimately come from God. We can never be independent of God. If we are seeking to love and serve God, there is no room for vanity or conceit. There is no need to boast of our own achievements. Pride causes hatred and envy. Spiritual pride can prevent us from recognising sin, and reduces any hope of repentance. "Lord, all that I am, and all that I have, comes from you. Give me a humble and grateful heart, through Christ our Lord."

The Sin of Envy. To envy someone is to resent their good fortune. Envy disturbs our peace of mind, and causes jealousy or discontent. It can develop into other sins. "Love your neighbour as yourself" is the Second Commandment. "Lord, thank you for your many blessings. Lord, I pray for ...... and ask you to bless and guide ...... in all things, through Jesus Christ our Lord."

The Sin of Anger. Anger is the opposite of Christian love. Rage and uncontrolled anger are dangerous, and hurt other people, whether through words, actions or silence. People sometimes respond with angry words or actions. There is good or righteous anger, which is a reaction to evil. Jesus was angry with the money-changers in the Temple. Righteous anger can be aroused by cruelty or abuse to people or animals. Remember the words of Saint Paul: "Let not the sun go down on your wrath." Anger becomes sinful when we want to retaliate or hurt someone. "O Lord, forgive my anger, and help me to know your peace."

The Sin of Greed. This is a powerful longing, especially for wealth, which is never satisfied. The sin of greed can lead to lack of compassion and hardness of heart. "You cannot serve God and money." To overcome greed, learn to be happy and satisfied with what you have. "Lord, thank you for your many blessings, and help me to be more generous to others."

The Sin of Gluttony. God has given us the instinct to eat and drink, which is good in itself. Excessive eating and drinking abuses God's gifts and also causes health problems. Drunkenness causes misery as well as ruining lives. Moderation and self-restraint should keep pleasures within proper limits. "Lord, help me to develop self control, and learn to say No." When gluttony is caused by stress or a problem, is there a better remedy for it, other than excessive food and drink?

The Sin of Lust. God has given us powerful sexual desires, which are good in themselves. Lust is a strong desire for unlawful and unrestrained sexual pleasure. There is widespread sexual freedom in many countries. But sex outside marriage is still a sin for a Christian, and it can split families and cause endless unhappiness. "Blest are the pure in heart, for they shall see our God." Your body is a temple of the Holy Spirit. Guard against any occasion which will lead to sin. "Lord, purify my desires, and send your blessing on … "

The Sin of Sloth. Sloth is both extreme physical and spiritual laziness, a complete lack of motivation. "The Devil finds work for idle hands." Spiritual sloth leads to slackness in worship, prayer and Bible reading. The opposite of sloath is zeal. To overcome spiritual slackness – try to remember where your spiritual journey is leading you – to God. He is both Judge and loving Father. God wants our freely given response to His love for us. "Lord, fill me with your Spirit and give me grace to persevere to the end."

CHRISTIAN STEWARDSHIP

It is wise to think about this only when you are settled in your faith.

What is Christian Stewardship? We are not owners. We are only stewards – or managers – of all that God has given to us for our lifetime. Our duty is to use all God's gifts as God would have us use them. Christians try to live the whole of their lives according to God's will. There is no area of life outside the concern of God.

Our creation. Our life is a gift from God. We have done nothing to deserve or earn this gift. God is the Creator of all that exists. He alone keeps all life in existence. All that we have and all that we are is a trust from God. As stewards, we acknowledge that we own nothing, and that everything ultimately belongs to God.

Our redemption. The greatest gift which God has given to us is His Son Jesus. We can share in the very life of God through the death and resurrection of Jesus Christ. Our sins separate us from God. Christ's death on the Cross redeems us – saves us – from our sins.

How we respond to our creation and redemption. God looks to us for a response to what He has done for us. It is called Stewardship. It is about "giving back" to God a proportion of what He has first given to us. We can think about stewardship in three areas:

Stewardship of time. Some of us have more spare time than others. Life may proceed at a leisurely pace or a frantic rush. Leisure as well as work is important. If we really want to do something, time can usually be found. We all have our priorities and as one grows in the faith, so they change. We acknowledge that all our time is a gift from God by giving back a responsible proportion of it to Him.

Stewardship of skills and abilities. God gives some skills and abilities to everyone. He has given us a mind with which we can think, and a body with which we can work. To acknowledge and show appreciation for our gifts, we can offer back to God a proportion of our skills for His work.

Stewardship of Money. The way we use our money is a personal choice. In the society in which we live, it is a vital and integral part of our lives. Just as the Church here on earth needs our time, skills and abilities, so it needs our money. We have the need to give this money. It shows our commitment to God.

Giving money back to God through His Church is one way to say thank you to God for our creation and our "Redemption". Money can be seen in a sacramental way. It is the outward sign of our gratitude to God. Money is earned by the skills of mind and hands. It represents us.

The responsible use of money is a measure of our commitment to God. He wants us to give back to Him a reasonable proportion of our income. The Bible suggests that we give ten per cent of our income to God. That is a very high standard and cannot be achieved by many. Others think in terms of five per cent. We may not achieve this until we are well and truly established in the faith. It is for each of us to make our own response to God in this matter, and to give back what we consider is a worthy and responsible proportion of our income.

At the end of our lives, we hand everything back to God. We can say thank you by leaving something in a Bequest for God's work to continue through His Church.

Stewardship of the environment. The earth belongs to God. Proper care of the world is "good Christian stewardship" as well as common sense. Care and welfare of animals should also be included.

Christian Stewardship in the Bible. The best source for understanding Christian Stewardship is in the Scriptures. Here is a selection of appropriate verses:

Deuteronomy 16.17: "Every man shall give as he is able, according to the blessing of the Lord your God which He has given you."
Psalm 24.1: "The earth is the Lord's and the fullness thereof."
2 Corinthians 8.9: "You know the grace of our Lord Jesus Christ, that though He was rich, yet for your sake He became poor, so that by His poverty you might become rich."
1 Corinthians 16.1-2: "Now concerning the contribution for the saints. On the first day of every week, each of you is to put something aside."
1 Timothy 6.10: "The love of money is the root of all evils."
2 Corinthians 9.6: "He who sows sparingly will also reap sparingly, and he who sows bountifully will also reap bountifully."
St Luke 6.38: "The measure you give will be the measure you get back."

THE KINGDOM OF GOD

In the OT, God was King in Heaven. In the NT, Jesus begins His public ministry with these words. St Mark 1.15: "The time is fulfilled, and the Kingdom of God is at hand. Repent and believe in the Gospel." The whole of His public ministry was spent in teaching about the Kingdom, but it is not an easy subject to understand.

The Jewish idea of a Saviour. The Jews wanted a leader to throw out the Roman army. But God does not reign on earth in that way. There was a notice on the Cross – "Jesus of Nazareth, the King of the Jews," written in irony, but true. Jesus Christ reigns from the Cross.

What did Jesus mean by the Kingdom of God? It is not about fighting with military power. Jesus taught that the Kingdom of God is a spiritual Kingdom of justice. The Kingdom is found in human hearts where God is Lord. The Kingdom is a spiritual reality. It is a Kingdom of justice, truth and love. It is the task of the Church to spread these qualities in the world.

The Kingdom has already arrived. It arrived with the coming of Jesus. St Luke 17.21: "The Kingdom of God is in the midst of you." Jesus was not just a messenger who taught people about the Kingdom. He was Himself the Good News. He was and is the King.

The Kingdom is unseen. The Kingdom became a spiritual reality in a fuller sense through the self-offering of Jesus on the Cross. The Fourth Gospel regards the crucifixion as the coronation of Jesus. His sacrificial death made it possible for us to enter into His Kingdom.

The Kingdom of God has already come. The Kingdom came with the coming of Jesus Christ. But it is also a hidden Kingdom.

The Kingdom will come in the future. The Creed says – "He will come again to judge the living and the dead." The Church connects this Second Coming with a belief in the "resurrection of the body and the life everlasting." The Kingdom will only then be fully revealed.

Jesus taught about the Kingdom in Parables. In fact, the central theme of Our Lord's teaching is the Kingdom of God. He showed us different aspects of God's reign on earth.

The parables Jesus told were simple stories. They held the listeners attention and wonderfully illustrated the point He was making. Here are some examples:

The Parable of the Sower. (St Matthew 13.4-23; St Mark 4.3-20; St Luke 8.5-15). Christ is the Sower. The seed is the living Word of God. The soil is those who hear God's Word. God's Kingdom grows when people hear and receive the message, and respond to it according to their spiritual awareness.

The Prodigal (lost) son. (St Luke 15.11-32). A son leaves a happy home, taking his inheritance with him. When the money runs out, he comes home. The parable shows us how God in His love will always welcome repentant sinners into His Kingdom.

The Good Samaritan. (St Luke 10.25-37). A man is robbed and wounded on the road to Jericho. A Jewish priest and a Levite (one who assists in the Temple) both passed him by on the other side of the road. But a hated Samaritan helped him in his time of need. Jesus asks – "Which of the three proved neighbour to the man who fell among the robbers?" He is really telling us that there are no limits to love in the Kingdom of God.

The Kingdom. Jesus never left us a crystal clear description of the Kingdom. Here are two glimpses – but there are many other examples:

St Luke 13.18-21: Jesus said – "What is the Kingdom of God like? And to what shall I compare it? It is like a grain of mustard seed, which a man took and sowed in his garden; and it grew and became a tree, and the birds of the air made nests in its branches."

And again He said, "To what shall I compare the Kingdom of God? It is like leaven which a woman took and hid in three measures of meal, till it was all leavened."

The Kingdom of Love. Jesus is concerned about our quality of life here on earth, and our relationship with other people. He wants His followers to show Christian qualities not only in holiness, but also in compassion and care for other people. He is really telling us that His Kingdom is open to all who will respond to His love.

THE FOUR LAST THINGS

The Four Last Things are Death, Judgement, Heaven and Hell. For centuries, the Church has gathered certain insights into the subject. But St Paul reminds us in 1 Corinthians 2.9: "What eye has not seen, nor ear heard, nor the heart of man conceived, what God has prepared for those who love Him." In our earthly life, it is a mystery of God.

Death. Many people avoid thinking about death, and what follows. That is short sighted and not wise. Death is the only thing which is certain to happen in this life.

The soul leaves the body when we die. The body turns to dust. It sleeps until the General Resurrection of the dead.

Particular Judgement. At death, the soul comes immediately into the light of God's presence. God's perfect light shows up and judges all our failures and sins. Then there is a time of waiting before the General Resurrection. During this time, the state of the soul depends on how it is judged in the pure light of God.

Purgatory. When we come through the gate of death, most people still need to be purified of their sins. Compared with the holiness of God, we are not holy. We have the same relationship with God immediately after death as we had with Him while we were still alive. We need to be purified. Hence we pray for those who have died.

The Second Coming of Christ. The First Coming of Christ was with great humility, when God emptied Himself of His glory. His Second Coming will be with glory and power, and He will judge both the living and the dead.

The General Resurrection of the dead. The soul will return to the body. The soul and resurrected spiritual body will be united again in eternal life. It will be a spiritual body, and not a human body as it was on earth. It will be free from temptation and sin.
1 Thessalonians 4.16: "The dead in Christ will rise first. Then we who are alive, who are left, shall be caught up together with them in the clouds, and meet the Lord in the air. And so we shall always be with the Lord."

The Communion of Saints. There is a "community life" in the Holy Trinity. It is a perfect communion and fellowship and sharing of a life of love between Father, Son and Holy Spirit. This communion and fellowship is shared with the OT Prophets and Patriarchs, the Blessed Virgin Mary, the Apostles, Saints and Martyrs. It includes all who have died in a state of grace and friendship with God.

Heaven. Jesus Christ opened the door into Heaven through His precious death and resurrection. Through our Baptism, we are united with the death and resurrection of Christ. Those who put their trust in Him are one day brought into the glory and happiness of Heaven.

What is Heaven like? Jesus does not give us a simple description of Heaven. Instead, we are given a number of different pictures:

Revelations 7.9: "After this, I looked, and behold, a great multitude which no man could number, from every nation, from all tribes and peoples and tongues, standing before the throne and before the Lamb, clothed in white robes, with palm branches in their hands, and crying with a loud voice, "Salvation belongs to our God who sits upon the throne, and to the Lamb."
St John 14.2: "In my Father's house are many rooms; if it were not so, would I have told you that I go to prepare a place for you? And when I go and prepare a place for you, I will come again and will take you to myself, that where I am you may be also."
St John 11.25: Jesus said, "I am the resurrection and the life; he who believes in me, though he die, yet shall he live, and whoever lives and believes in me shall never die."
See also 1 Corinthians 15; Philippians 3.21; St Matthew 22.31;
St John 6.35-40; Romans 8.31-9 and 14.7-9; Revelation 21.1-7.

Hell. This is the destination or state of those who finally reject the love of God. Anyone who tries to love God will be given sufficient grace to go to Heaven. God has given us free will. He has given each person a real choice to accept His love, or to reject it. The decision of those who reject God will be respected, and they will go to Hell.

What is Hell like? This is difficult to answer. Some believe that the flames of Hell described in the NT are only picture language. Certainly Hell is a deliberate separation from God.

DOES GOD WANT YOU TO BE A PRIEST?

Some men are called to be full time priests, and paid by the Church. Others are called to be "Non-stipendiary" priests who earn a living at their usual job, and help with priestly duties by arrangement when possible.

Selection process for the Sacred Ministry. Every inward call has to be tested and approved by the Church. This is important, because a priest is a representative of the universal Church, as well as a representative of Christ. It is the Bishop who decides who will or will not be ordained. Bishops have people to help in the selection process. Each candidate goes through a diocesan selection, which differs from diocese to diocese. If recommended, the candidate attends a Selection Conference arranged on a national basis. This is an opportunity to meet others who are thinking about ordination, and are in the process of having it tested.

Each candidate has to have five references, and a medical report. Selection Conferences are held at a variety of locations, and usually at Diocesan Retreat Houses. They last from Monday evening to Friday. There are normally sixteen candidates and six Selectors. There is a Eucharist and Evensong every day, and various interviews, discussions and tests. The Selector's decision has to be unanimous. They usually take 24 hours after the departure of the candidates to reach their decisions. They make reports to the Bishops as "advice", which the Bishops usually (but not always) accept.

Training for the Sacred Ministry. This is done as a full time student at a college, or alternatively on a "Course" at a convenient local centre. Course students do their normal jobs during the day and study at home in the evening. They attend lectures and discussions at weekends during term time. A course usually lasts three years.

Ordination. Authority to exercise the office and ministry of a Priest comes from God alone, through the Sacrament of Ordination. This involves the laying on of hands with prayer by the bishop and other priests, on the head of each candidate. There is a saying – "Once a priest, always a priest". Ordination imprints a character which is indelible and cannot be removed. Thus great care is taken in the selection process. Saint Paul wrote "Lay hands on no man suddenly".

The Ministry of a Priest. There is only one priest, Jesus Christ. Every priest shares in His Priesthood. Priests are called to be an 'icon' or image of Christ. He must stand at the altar and offer the Eucharist as the representative of Christ. Christ gave authority and power to the priest to forgive and absolve sins in His name. He administers Baptism, and prepares candidates for Confirmation. He is a Leader, but also a Servant. He proclaims the Word of God and expounds its meaning. He must assimilate the Scriptures into his own life. He is a Shepherd who cares for the sick, dying and bereaved. He must share the love of God with other people. He is a man of faith, who shares his faith with others.

Responsibilities of the Parish. It is good to ask when the parish last produced a candidate for ordination? A priest is usually on the look-out for people with vocations.

God's "Call" comes in different ways. It may be a nagging idea at the back of your mind which will not go away, or a "still small voice". It may be a complete surprise. It may be an unwelcome idea, but if you feel God is calling you, discuss it with your priest.

The Call of the Prophet Isaiah. I said, "Woe is me. For I am lost. For I am a man of unclean lips, and I dwell in the midst of a people of unclean lips; for my eyes have seen the King, the Lord of Hosts. Then flew one of the seraphim to me, having in his hand a burning coal which he had taken with tongs from the altar. He touched my mouth, and said, "Behold. This has touched your lips; your guilt is taken away, and your sin forgiven." I heard the voice of the Lord saying, "Whom shall I send, and who will go for us?" Then I said, "Here am I. Send me." (Isaiah 6.1-8)

Vocations in the Bible. It helps to read about the call of some great figures in the Bible. Here is a selection, but there are many others. Compare them with your own thoughts, fears, prayers and struggles:

The call of Abram (Abraham) – Genesis 12.1-2.
The call of Moses – Exodus 3.1-12.
The call of the boy Samuel – 1 Samuel 3.1-19.
The call of Jeremiah – Jeremiah 1.4-10.
The call of Saul (St Paul) – Acts of the Apostles 9.1-19.

THE ROYAL PRIESTHOOD OF ALL WHO ARE BAPTISED

God may not want you to be an "ordained" priest. But He does have work for each and every member of His Church. Baptism and Confirmation are a consecration and commitment to God. He invites all the passengers on His Ship of Salvation to turn into crew members, who, in the course of time, are able to help the other passengers.

Christ calls each of us: "Come, follow me". When our souls have been touched by God, we respond and try to develop our spiritual lives. We try to grow in our knowledge and love of God. We belong to the Church because we have faith in Christ, and we seek a more intimate relationship with Him through prayer, adoration and the Eucharist.

It is not enough to be concerned only with our own spiritual relationship with God. Christ places the continuation of His work in the hands of ordinary Christians. He calls us to proclaim the Gospel to other people mainly by the kind of lives we live. We should try to live our lives according to the Gospel. Could we go so far as to say – other people should be able to see something of Christ in our daily lives? God wants our faith to be passed on to our children, and to our children's children – and of course, to our neighbours. There comes a time when we realise that we have a responsibility in this matter.

It is a vital part of God's plan that we learn how to pass on our faith, and not to keep it to ourselves. There is a problem. Most people do not know how to do this. Perhaps we are frightened or embarrassed. We would all agree that we have something precious, which is worth sharing. Whether by word or deed, we are called to do our best in this. A small sacrifice on our part can often be a great help with God's work. We become a "changed people" and transformed into His likeness. The quality of our lives is important. Actions speak louder than words. But occasionally, you may be asked to put your faith into words. An easy way to do this is simply to tell your own 'faith' story: "Let me tell you how I first came to faith in God and then to Church."

Jesus made sure that His mission and ministry could continue in the future through ordinary Church members. If we are to do our share in this, then we have to listen to what God is hoping to say to us. Reflecting on the meaning of the following may be helpful:

The Royal Priesthood of all who are baptised. Saint Peter wrote (1 Peter 2.4-6): "Come to Him, to that living stone, rejected by men but in God's sight chosen and precious; and like living stones, be yourselves built into a spiritual house, to be a holy priesthood, to offer spiritual sacrifices acceptable to God through Jesus Christ."

"The Church is the only organisation which exists for those who do not belong". (Archbishop William Temple).

"All authority in Heaven and on earth has been given to me. Go therefore and make disciples of all nations, baptising them in the name of the Father and of the Son and of the Holy Spirit, teaching them to observe all that I have commanded you. And lo, I am with you always, to the close of the age." (St Matthew 28.18-20). Jesus spoke these words just before His Ascension. He places the continuation of His work in our hands.

"To Him who loves us and has freed us from our sins by His blood, and made us a kingdom, priests to His God and Father, to Him be glory and dominion for ever and ever." So wrote St John the Divine to the seven Churches that are in Asia. (Revelation 1.6)

"Do you not know that you are God's temple, and that God's Spirit dwells in you?" (1 Corinthians 3.16). God is ever with us to help us.

"You are the salt of the earth." (St Matthew 5.13)

"Be ye doers of the Word, and not hearers only, deceiving yourselves." (St James 1.22)

"Faith by itself, if it has no works, is dead." (St James 2.17)

"Love your neighbour as yourself."

"Am I my brother's keeper?" (Genesis 4.9) The answer is Yes.

We are called to be "Ambassadors for Christ".

"You are the Body of Christ and individually members of it." (1 Corinthians 12.27)

ANCIENT SIGNS AND CUSTOMS

God took flesh and became human in Jesus. So it is appropriate to use all our bodily senses in worship – sight, smell, hearing, touch and taste.

The Sign of the Cross. This is made by moving the right hand from the forehead to the stomach, and then from the left shoulder to the right. While making the sign of the Cross, we say "In the name of the Father, and of the Son, and of the Holy Spirit. Amen". It is a prayer in action, which sums up the central act of our faith. (1) It shows the nature of God as three Persons in One God. (2) It reminds us that Christ died on the Cross to save us from our sins. (3) It shows that we belong to Christ and His Church. The Sign of the Cross is also made when the Gospel is announced, at the Absolution, at the beginning of the Sermon, at the Benedictus (Blessed is he who comes in the name of the Lord), before receiving both the Body and Blood of Christ, and at the Blessing.

Genuflection. We worship God with our bodies as well as in "Spirit and in truth." The Prayer Book (1662): "And here we offer and present unto Thee, O Lord, ourselves, our souls and bodies to be a reasonable, holy and lively sacrifice unto Thee." Saint Paul wrote: "At the name of Jesus every knee shall bow" (Philippians 2.10). Genuflecting is a sign of respect, honour and reverence at the real presence of Christ in the Eucharist. We genuflect in the following places – when coming into a Church where the Blessed Sacrament is reserved in an Aumbry or Tabernacle – in the Creed when we say "and was made Man" (to show the reality and greatness of God taking human flesh) – and just before and after receiving Communion. We need outward gestures to show what we believe inwardly in our hearts.

Colours of the Church Year. There is a special colour for each Season, Festival or Saints Day. The colour of the Priest's Vestments, Stole, Altar Frontal and Pulpit Fall change as follows -
White or gold is used for the Festivals of Christ e.g. Christmas, Easter, Ascension.
Red reminds us of fire or blood. It is used at Pentecost (tongues of fire) and for Saints whose blood was shed for Christ.
Purple or violet – the colour for Lent and Advent – seasons of penitence and preparation.
Green is used when there is no special Season, Festival, or Saints Day.

Stole. A long narrow scarf (worn by priests and deacons). Colour varies according to Season or Saints Day. The stole (and girdle) represent the cords used to bind Jesus when He was arrested.

Chasuble. The outer garment worn by a Priest in the Eucharist. It represents the seamless robe worn by Christ before His Crucifixion. It is often decorated with a Cross, which reminds the Priest that he must carry the Cross to follow Christ. Sometimes the Cross is in the shape of a "Y" and this represents the arms of Christ on the Cross.

Incense. Incense is the resins and gums extracted from certain trees and plants. It is burned with charcoal (in a thurible or censer) to produce a perfumed smoke. Good worship should involve our whole beings, including our senses such as sight and smell. The incense represents the prayers of the faithful ascending to Heaven. It gives a sense of awe and mystery to the sacrifice of the Eucharist.

The Bible has many references to the use of incense. In the OT, the prophet Isaiah had a vision of God, and "the house was filled with smoke". (Isaiah 6.4). In the NT, the Wise Men "offered Him gifts, gold and frankincense and myrrh" (St Matthew 2.11). Zechariah "was on duty, and it fell to him by lot to enter the Temple of the Lord and burn incense". (St Luke 1.11). St Paul wrote: "We are indeed the incense offered by Christ to God, both for those who are on the way to salvation, and for those who are on the way to perdition: to the latter it is a deadly fume that kills, to the former a vital fragrance that brings life" (2 Corinthians 2.15 NEB). Incense is used in the vision of the worship of Heaven: "Another angel stood at the altar with the golden censer, and he was given much incense to mingle with the prayers of all the saints upon the golden altar before the throne; and the smoke of the incense rose with the prayers of the saints before God" (Revelation 8.3-4).

When is incense used? The Altar is censed at the beginning of the Eucharist. The Gospel is censed before it is read. It is used at the offertory to show that the most solemn part of the service is about to begin. The oblations of bread and wine, and the altar, are censed. Then priest and congregation are censed. The congregation bow to the Thurifer as he approaches, and again after the congregation has been censed.

GLOSSARY OF UNUSUAL WORDS

Abba. An Aramaic word meaning Father or Daddy. Jesus used it to address His Heavenly Father.

Absolution. The words of forgiveness pronounced by the Priest.

Canon. Title of a priest at a cathedral.

Canon of the Mass. The Prayer to consecrate the bread and wine.

Canon of Scripture. List of books accepted by the Church as Sacred Scripture.

Creed. An official statement of the beliefs of the Church.

Deacon. One who holds the first degree of holy orders, which usually but not always leads on to the priesthood.

Diocese. Parishes grouped under the authority of a bishop.

Ecumenism. Working for Christian unity.

Episcopal Church. A Church with duly ordained bishops (eg Roman Catholic, Orthodox, Anglican, Old Catholic).

Evangelical. Christians for whom the Bible is the main source of authority.

Evangelism. Telling the Good News of God's love in Jesus Christ.

Fundamentalist. One who believes that the Scriptures are without error.

Gospel. The Good News of God's love in Jesus Christ. There are four accounts of the Gospel in the NT.

Heresy. A departure from orthodox belief.

High Priest. Head of the Jewish Temple at Jerusalem (destroyed 70AD). Jesus is the new High Priest in the Epistle to the Hebrews.

Incarnation. God took human flesh and became man to save the world.

Judaism. The religion of the Jews.

Litany. A general prayer with responses. Often sung.

Liturgy. Means an act of worship, or specifically the Eucharist.

Mattins. Morning act of worship with psalms, canticles and readings, now mainly used as the priest's "Daily Office".

Metropolitan Bishop. An archbishop presiding over a Province (group of dioceses) eg Canterbury, York.

Mission. The spreading of the Christian faith and the whole work of the Church.

Monotheism. Belief in one God (Christianity, Islam and Judaism).

Myth. Truth which is passed on through a story.

Penitence. Sorrow for sin.

Polytheism. Religions which worship many "gods".

Rabbi. A teacher of the Jewish faith.

Reformation. Martin Luther protested against abuses in the Church in 1517. Protestant Churches broke away from the authority of Rome.

Son of Man. Jesus called himself the Son of Man.

Synagogue. A Jewish place of worship, found in most cities today.

Temple. The centre of Jewish worship in Jerusalem (until 70AD).

Trinity. The belief that there are Three Persons – Father, Son and Holy Spirit – in the One God. (Unitarians reject this belief).

Vatican. Main residence of the Pope in Rome. Centre of RC Church.

FIRST SUGGESTION FOR DAILY PRAYER

Preparation: + Make the sign of the Cross.

In the name of the Father, and of the Son, and of the Holy Spirit.

O Holy Sprit of God, come and assist us in our prayers. (PAUSE)

Adoration:

Most holy and eternal Trinity, Father, Son and Holy Spirit,
I worship and praise and adore you
With all my heart and mind and soul and strength.
To you be praise and glory, for time and for eternity. (PAUSE)

Confession:

O Lord, I confess that I have sinned in thought and word and deed,
And in what I have failed to do.
I am very sorry for my sins by which I have offended you.
I resolve by the help of your grace not to sin again. (PAUSE)

Lord, have mercy;   Christ, have mercy;   Lord, have mercy.

Thanksgiving:

Lord, I thank you for your forgiveness and love. I thank you for …
Lord, you have given so much to us. Give us one thing more, a thankful
heart, for Christ's sake. Amen. (PAUSE)

Supplications:

Lord, I offer all that I will think, speak or do this day to you
OR I offer all that I have thought, spoken and done this day to you

The Lord's Prayer.   Our Father, who art in Heaven ……

Ending: The Lord bless us, and keep us from all evil, and bring us to
everlasting life. Amen.

SECOND SUGGESTION FOR DAILY PRAYER

Make the Sign of the Cross and say –

+ In the name of the Father, and of the Son, and of the Holy Spirit. Amen.

Adoration

Glory be to the Father and to the Son and to the Holy Spirit; as it was in the beginning, is now, and ever shall be, world without end. Amen.

Use in Lent and Advent – instead of the Gloria

Holy God, Holy and strong, Holy and immortal, have mercy on us.

Reading from the Bible: A Psalm and/or Gospel may be used.

Ave Maria

Hail Mary, full of grace, the Lord is with Thee.
Blessed art thou among women,
and blessed is the fruit of thy womb, Jesus.
Holy Mary, Mother of God, pray for us sinners,
now and at the hour of our death.

Intercessions – (develop your own relationship with God)

O Lord, I thank you for … and for your love in Jesus.
I offer this day to you … and all my thoughts and words and deeds.
Send your Holy Spirit, and bless and guide ……..

The Lord's Prayer: Our Father, who art in Heaven

Ending

+ May the Divine Assistance remain with us, now and always, and may the souls of the faithful, through the mercy of God, rest in peace.

A SELECTION OF PRAYERS

The Jesus Prayer

Lord Jesus Christ, Son of the living God,
have mercy on us miserable sinners.

The Angelus

> The angel of the Lord appeared to Mary
> And she conceived by the Holy Spirit.

Hail Mary, full of grace, the Lord is with Thee. Blessed art thou among
Women, and blessed is the fruit of thy womb, Jesus. Holy Mary, Mother
of God, pray for us sinners, now and at the hour of our death.

> Behold, the handmaid of the Lord,
> Be it unto me according to thy word.

Hail Mary, full of grace (as above)

> The Word was made flesh, and dwelt among us.

Hail Mary, full of grace (as above)

> Pray for us, O holy Mother of God
> That we may be made worthy of the promises of Christ.

Pour forth, we beseech Thee, O Lord, Thy grace into our hearts;
That as we have known the incarnation of Thy Son Jesus Christ by the
Message of an angel, + so by His Cross and passion we may be brought
to the glory of His resurrection, through Jesus Christ our Lord. Amen.

Te Deum (first part)

We praise Thee, O God; we acknowledge Thee to be the Lord.
All the earth doth worship Thee: the Father everlasting.
To Thee all angels cry aloud: the Heavens and all the Powers therein.
To Thee Cherubim and Seraphim continually do cry,
Holy, Holy, Holy, Lord God of Sabaoth,
Heaven and earth are full of the majesty of Thy glory.
The glorious company of the Apostles praise Thee.
The goodly fellowship of the Prophets praise Thee.
The noble army of Martyrs praise Thee.
The holy Church throughout all the world doth acknowledge Thee.
The Father of an infinite majesty;
Thine honourable, true and only Son;
Also the Holy Spirit the Comforter.

A Prayer for more Priests:

Almighty God, give us Priests:
To establish the honour of your holy name;
To offer the holy sacrifice of the altar;
To give us Jesus in the holy sacrament;
To proclaim the faith of Jesus;
To tend your sheep;
To seek the lost;
To give pardon to the penitent sinner;
To bless our homes;
To pray for the afflicted;
To comfort mourners;
To strengthen us in our last hour;
To commend our souls.
Almighty God, give us Priests.

Holy Father, you gave us Christ as the Shepherd of our souls;
may your people always have priests who care for them
with His great love.
We make our prayer through Jesus Christ, our Lord, who lives and
reigns with you and the Holy Spirit, One God for ever and ever. Amen.

A Prayer for the Church:

Father, you sent Saint Augustine to the people of England
To proclaim the faith delivered to Saint Peter and the Apostles.
May the work he began be renewed in this land
and continue to prosper.
Lord, those who are divided you unite,
And those who are united you support.
Help us to live up to the call you have given us,
So that we may bear witness to the truth
And strive that all believers may be united
in the bond of peace and love.

Mary, Mother of God and Mother of the Church, pray for us.
Saint Gregory the Great, pray for us.
Saint Augustine of Canterbury, pray for us.
Saint Thomas Becket, pray for us.

PRAYING FOR OTHER PEOPLE

To love your neighbour as yourself requires you to pray for them. Here are some suggestions. Perhaps you may wish to make your own list?

Daily Prayer: "Lord, bless and guide......our Bishop and the parishes and people in his care; and also ....our Priest and St.......'s Church".

Day of the month: O Lord, today I pray for ....

1 Peace and justice in the world (especially in ....)
2 Leaders of the nations (especially....)
3 All involved in local and national government.
4 Scientists. Those involved in scientific and medical research.
5 Writers. Journalists. All involved in broadcasting and entertainment
6 Police, Prison and Probation Officers. Their families.
7 Members of the Armed Forces. Their families. Service Chaplains.
8 Prisioners. Their families. Hostages. Those who captured them.
9 The Royal Family.
10 All who are disabled. Their families. Those who care for them.
11 All who are unemployed. All who are employed. Their families.
12 The poor and needy of the world. Homeless People. Refugees.
13 All who are retired. The elderly. The infirm.
14 Young families. Single Parents. All who live alone. Teenagers.
15 All who are separated or divorced. Children of broken homes.
16 The safety of unborn children. Midwives.
17 All who are married. The strengthening of home and family life.
18 Victims of crime. Those who care for them.
19 Students, staff and governors of schools, colleges and universities.
20 All who work in commerce, industry and finance.
21 Leaders in industry. All Trades Union officials and members.
22 All in charge of public transport. All who travel by land, air or sea
23 Those who help to maintain the life of the local community.
24 All who are blind. Their families. Those who care for them.
25 Doctors. Surgeons. Nurses. Hospital and Hospice staff and patients.
26 Drug addicts. Their families. All who help them.
27 All with an incurable disease. Their families. All who help them.
28 Funeral directors. Cemetery and crematorium staff. All who mourn.
29 All who work during the night.
30 The deaf. Their families. All who care for them.
31 Criminals and wicked people, that their hearts be turned to good.